100 Ideas

FOR STATIONERY, CARDS, AND INVITATIONS

100 Ideas

FOR STATIONERY, CARDS, AND INVITATIONS

GLOUCESTER MASSACHUSETTS

QUARRY BOOKS

Simple and Stylish
Projects Using Handmade
and Digital Techniques

LAURA MCFADDEN

To my loving husband, Matthew, my rock, thanks for putting up with me.
To my son, Ray, whom I love to pieces.
I cannot imagine how I managed to get through life before you.

First published in the United States of America by

Quarry Books, a member of
Quayside Publishing Group
33 Commercial Street
Gloucester, Massachusetts
01930-5089

Telephone: (978) 282-9590
Fax: (978) 283-2742
www.rockpub.com

McFadden, Laura.
  100 ideas for stationery, cards, and invitations : simple and stylish projects using handmade and digital techniques / Laura McFadden.
      p.   cm.
  Includes index.
  ISBN 1-59253-243-8 (pbk.)
  1. Greeting cards. 2. Invitation cards. 3. Computer art. I. Title.
  TT872.M333 2006
  745.594'1–dc22

                                                                                    2005027632
                                                                                    CIP

ISBN-13: 978-1-59253-243-8
ISBN-10: 1-59253-243-8

10 9 8 7 6 5 4 3 2 1

Design: Laura McFadden Design, Inc.
laura.mcfadden@rcn.com
Photography: Allan Penn
Templates and Illustrations:
Anna Herrick, Laura McFadden
Production: Laura McFadden,
Anna Herrick, and Joanna Detz

Printed in Singapore

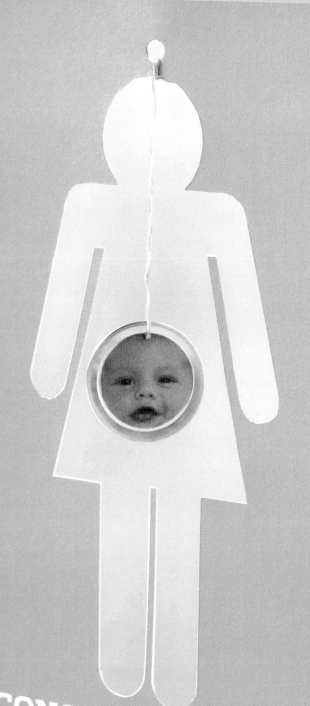

CONGRATULATIONS

Cut Out for Motherhood

Contents

Lady Liberty Tin with Stationery, page 117

2 >> Designing by Hand

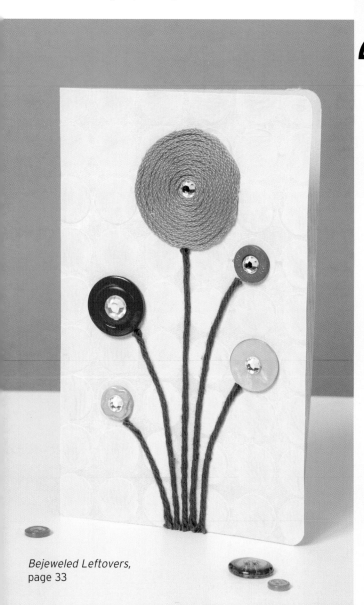

Bejeweled Leftovers, page 33

Oh Beehive! Card,
page 72

3 >> Hybrid Designs
Using Both the Computer and Handmade Techniques

4 >> Digital Designs
Computer-Generated Designs

Cantaloupe- and Melon-Colored Paper Message Cards, page 23

The inclination to write and to communicate is a universal characteristic of humankind, and as a child, I was no exception. At the tender age of two, I decided to try and communicate the best way I knew how. I grabbed a nail, toddled over to my next door neighbors', the Bartsches', 1920s-style house, and started to etch a design of my very own into their lovely slate blue-colored aluminum siding.

I graduated from the nail and aluminum siding to computer paper. In the early '60s, my dad worked at a telecommunications firm with computers the size of a living room. Out of these behemoth machines came reams of green and white striped paper printed with cryptic messages I later learned were Fortran code. Holes along the sides helped guide the paper through the print feeders. Every so often, my dad would come home to our small, suburban home in southern New Jersey with stacks of the used paper, and the seven McFadden rug rats would come out of the woodwork to draw and write on the white side of the sheets. Mom and Dad received many a holiday card with some random image and message crayoned onto this recycled computer paper.

Later on, I was able to upgrade my writing stock and purchase my very own Holly Hobbie and Scratch 'n' Sniff stationery, as well as a host of others with kitschy designs that I can barely remember.

Introduction

In art school in the 1980s, my friends would send me the wackiest letters, each person trying to outdo the next in being original. My friend Marc would photocopy his personal treasures onto white sheets of paper while he wrote hypergraphic volumes about everything going on in his life.

My boyfriend, Kevin, would send me letters completely typed up and formal, albeit the unfortunate blobs of Wite Out, which he used to cover up his typos.

The strangest letter I received was from Houston, Texas. My friend Lisa sent around a chain letter containing a 2" (5 cm) Palmetto bug meant to give us living (well, dead) proof about the size of the creatures she was cohabitating with down South.

Most likely, you too have fond memories of the unique correspondence you have received in the past, and like me, continue to enjoy sending personalized messages to your favorite people. You may not be writing letters containing Palmetto bugs, but hopefully this book will give you some great ideas for creating distinctive correspondence. Whether you want to use simple art supplies and embellishments or use your computer to aid in your creations, the projects shown here offer a wide array of designs and general techniques. Either take the designs directly, or use the book as a springboard to get your own creative juices flowing.

And, Mr. and Mrs. Bartsch, if you happen to see this book, sorry about the siding.

Laura McFadden

1 >> Getting Started

Striped Gesso Cards, page 25

The Basics: getting the supplies you need to get started

Here are some of the bare essentials you will need to work on any of the projects in this book. See individual projects for the full list.

Adhesives

Glue Stick A glue stick is fabulous for adhering a sheet of paper to another, and it is acid-free. This means your stationery or card will not develop yellow acidic stains. Glue sticks are not good for adhering little embellishments onto a sheet of paper.

Craft Glue This adhesive is good for gluing embellishments such as yarn, sequins, and buttons onto your project. It's not so great for gluing two sheets of paper together because it can dry lumpy.

Spray Adhesives Generally these work well for gluing two flat sheets together. You should use an extremely well-ventilated area and follow the manufacturer's warnings on the container. Also, many spray adhesives are not archival safe nor acid-free, which could cause your sheet to stains or yellow as time passes.

Tape You can always use tape while you are at work on these projects. It's an important staple for the crafter's work area.

Cutting Tools

Craft Knife Craft knives are a must-have for every paper crafter. These knives are great for cutting free-form images as well as straight edges. The blades must be changed frequently for optimal cutting. Use caution while using; the blades are sharp. Look for knives that have a roll-free lip around it for added safety.

Scissors They are great for cutting thread, yarn, freeform shapes, and much more and are a standard for craft projects.

Rotary Paper Trimmer A rotary paper trimmer is a great investment. Make a straight edge, a deckled edge, or a pinking-sheared edge all with a quick change of a blade. These trimmers are sold with a straight edge blade and other blades can be purchased separately.

Punches There are many projects in this book that call for a variety of punches. Circle and corner punches are great options for a really refined looking shape.

Drill Punch Want to make a hole in the middle of a page? A drill punch allows you to make a hole anywhere on a page and not be limited to the edges.

Measuring Tools

Metal Ruler Using a metal ruler allows you to cut straight edges with precision as well measure your project.

Triangle Use a triangle as an easy way to square up the edge of your paper and get a perpendicular cut.

Work Surfaces

Cutting Mat A self-healing cutting mat is a great way to save your tables from getting scratched. You can use them over and over again because the mat self-heals, leaving no visible traces of your incisions from the project.

Work Table When crafting, use a surface that you don't mind getting beat up! A folding table with some brown paper covering the surface works well.

Spin Art Cards, page 21

Choosing a Winning Combination of Colors and Papers

The skinny on picking the best colors, styles, and combinations

Do you often leave a stationery supply store with nothing in hand? Purchasing paper can be an overwhelming and sometimes expensive endeavor. While there is no scientific method to doing all of this, there are some techniques for picking out the best selection for you.

Fashion Statement Custom Envelope and Stationery, page 121; *Needles and Pins Notecard,* page 32; *Bejeweled Leftovers,* page 33

1. Get a Concept Drawing a little sketch before you get to the store can help you visualize the project before you open your wallet and blow lots of money on paper you may not use. However, leaving your mind open to what you see at the supplier should not be overruled.

2. Get a Color Forecast Is brown the new black? Is purple the new pink? Is orange out? What's a trippy tint? Looking at a color forecast can help you figure out what the hot new colors are and how you might combine them for a winning look. Search online for color forecasts, and watch trendy gift and clothing catalogs for color ideas. One last thing to consider: Will you be able to write on the color you choose? You may need to purchase pens in metallic or light colors.

3. Mix and Match Paper manufacturers create papers with the understanding that you may want a polka-dotted envelope and a striped card. Look for sets of paper that are variations on a theme. These themed sets of paper may be all pastels, all embroidered, or all vibrant hues. Walk around the store with the sheet you are thinking about and place it next to other sheets in the store that are of a similar ilk.

4. Card Stock versus Text Weight Think about what paper weights you will need. You may not want a flimsy card, so your best bet may be to go with card stock. If you find paper you love but is too thin, you can always adhere it to some heavier weight paper. Conversely, you may not want to have a letter written on card stock, so text weight may be the way to go.

5. Quality Rules If you want a really nice result, you must start with good ingredients. Paper is no exception. Take a close look at the paper. How does it feel? Is the paper hand silk-screened, does it feel natural, or does it look chintzy? If you still have no idea, have a salesperson give you some advice.

The Envelope Size Please...

A quick chart of some standard (and not so standard) sized envelopes

Name	Size	Common Usage
STANDARD		
#1 baby	2 ¼" × 3 ½" (5.5 × 9 cm)	Business cards, tags, quick notes
4-bar	3 ⅝" × 5 ⅛" (9.5 × 13 cm)	Thank-you or small notes
A2	4 ⅜" × 5 ¾" (11 × 14.5 cm)	Quick note or invitation
A6	4 ¾" × 6 ½" (11.5 × 17 cm)	Cards, invitations, notecards, hangtags
A7	5 ¼" × 7 ¼" (13.5 × 18.5 cm)	Formal invitations and larger cards
A8	5 ½" × 8 ⅛" (14 × 20 cm)	Oversized cards
A9	5 ¾" × 8 ¾" (14.5 × 22.5 cm)	Bolder, bigger cards
BARONIAL		
2	3 ³⁄₁₆" × 4 ¼" (9 × 10.5 cm)	Formal correspondence, invitations, cards
4	3 ⅝" × 4 ⅝" (9.5 × 11.5 cm)	Formal correspondence
5	4 ⅛" × 5 ⅛" (10 × 13 cm)	Formal correspondence
5 ¼	4 ¼" × 5 ¼" (10.5 × 13.5 cm)	Formal correspondence
5 ½	4 ⅜" × 5 ⅝" (11 × 14.5 cm)	Formal correspondence
6	5" × 6 ¼" (13 × 15.5 cm)	Formal correspondence
MISCELLANEOUS		
#10	4 ⅛" × 9 ½" (10 × 24 cm)	Standard business correspondence
Presentation	9 ½" × 12 ½" (24 × 32 cm)	Fits an 8 ½" × 11" (22 × 28 cm) sheet
5 ¾" Square	5 ¾" × 5 ¾" (15 × 15 cm)	Modern invitations, cards
6 ½" Square	6 ½" × 6 ½" (17 × 17 cm)	Larger, modern invitations and cards

Tips and Techniques *Some basic instruction for the beginning crafter*

Squaring and Cutting Out a Sheet of Paper

While this is a very rudimentary step, it will make the difference between a tailored-looking end product or a homegrown one.

materials

- ~ metal ruler
- ~ triangle
- ~ craft knife
- ~ cutting mat
- ~ paper or card stock
- ~ pencil

1. Place a sheet of paper, decorative side down, on the cutting mat and measure out the size of paper you would like to end up with (for example: 4" × 6" [10 × 15 cm]). Use one of the corners of the sheet as a starting point.

2. Make light marks with a pencil at the desired vertical and horizontal measurements.

3. Align the triangle with the bottom edge of the paper and draw a vertical line with the pencil.

4. Align the triangle with the left edge of the paper and draw a horizontal line with the pencil until you have a rectangle drawn out.

5. Using the pencil lines you have just drawn as guides, cut the sheet out with a craft knife and metal ruler.

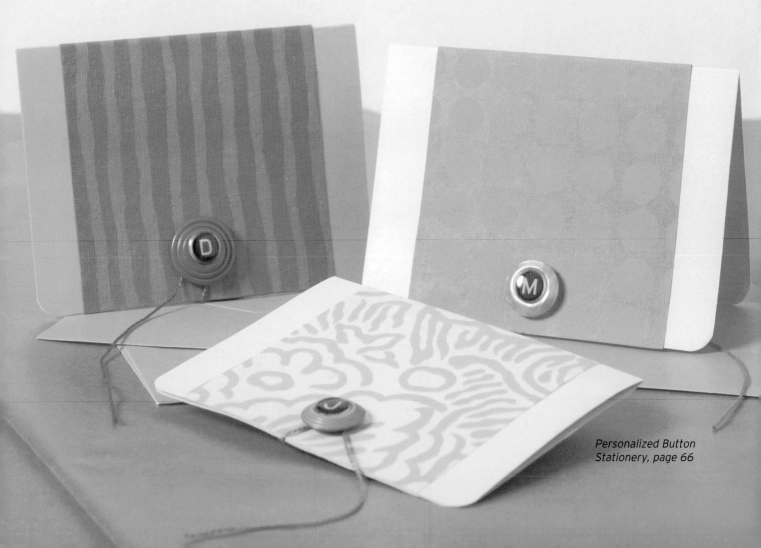

Personalized Button Stationery, page 66

Setting an Eyelet

1. Place your paper, decorative side up, on the cutting mat.

2. With a pencil, mark the center of the area where you would like the eyelet to appear.

3. Select a nib for the screw punch that best matches the size of your eyelet. Screw the nib into the handle and make a hole in the paper by bearing down on the handle with the palm of your hand. The twisting motion of the screw punch will create a hole in the paper similar to a hole punch. (The advantage of using this tool over the traditional hole punch is that you can make a hole anywhere on the page. Also, the ability to change the nibs to the size of the eyelet prevents the eyelet from slipping through the hole.)

4. Drop the eyelet into the hole you just made, keeping the "frame" side of the eyelet face up, with the decorative side of the paper also face up.

Procrastinator's Birthday Greeting, page 100

5. Flip the paper over, decorative side down, with the eyelet still in place. Place the eyelet-setting tool, pointed side down, into the middle of the hole on the back side of the eyelet.

6. Hit the end of the eyelet-setting tool several times with a hammer until the edges of the eyelet splay and lock into the sides of the paper.

materials

~ eyelet

~ eyelet-setting tool

~ hammer

~ screw punch

~ cutting mat

~ paper or card stock

~ pencil

Simple Sewn Stationery, page 107

Typesetting and Laying Out Pages

There are many software packages available to assist with the layout and typesetting of your invitations, cards, and stationery. Each one has its own set of tools and commands, which are customized for the individual programs. Most packages come with a tutorial or offer online training. Refer to your individual software for helpful information, or search the Web for more information.

Here are a few programs used in this book:
QuarkXPress
Microsoft Word
Photoshop

The ABCs of Typography *A quick terminology lesson on letterforms*

Ascender These are the necks of letters, or the part of the letter that points up. Lowercase letters such as b, l, and k are good examples of letters with ascenders.

Descender These are the tails of a letter, or the part of the letter that points down. The letters p, j, and g all have descenders.

Dingbat This is a small decorative mark, such as a bullet, small flower, or star, often used to divide, embellish, or emphasize certain key points. Zapf Dingbats or Woodtype Ornaments are common examples of dingbats.

Display Type This is decorative typography often used for headlines.

Justified Text that is aligned on both the left and right sides of a block of copy.

Kerning The space between letterforms. This helps make the type more attractive and, at times, more legible. Example of bad kerning: M ay is a beau tiful time of y ear. Example of good kerning: May is a beautiful time of year.

Leading The distance from the baseline of one line of type to the baseline of the following line of type.

Lowercase this is lowercase. the text has no capital letters.

Point Size This refers to the height of the characters on a page. This system of measurement was originally developed by type founder Pierre Fournier le Jeune in 1737 and its measurements were based on the total height of the metal type including leading (see leading).

Ragged Left Text that runs ragged, or uneven, on the left-hand side of the margin.

Example:

We will be coming

to the best party of

the twenty-first century

Ragged Right Text that runs ragged, or uneven, on the right-hand side of the margin.

Example:

We will be coming

to the best party of

the twenty-first century

Instant Messaging Index Card Gift Set, page 99

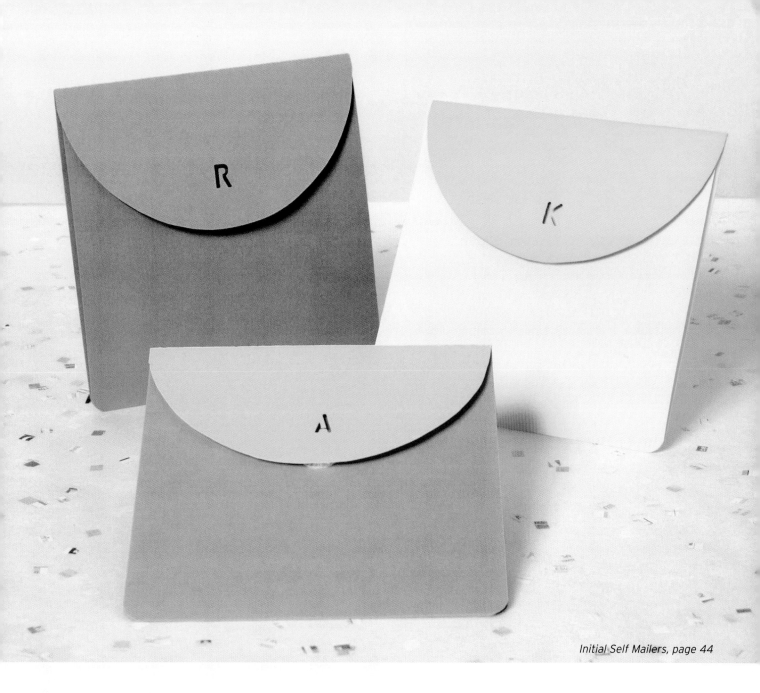

Initial Self Mailers, page 44

Sans Serif Type without the arms, tails, and stems on letters. This is a more modern form of typography. Fonts such as Helvetica and Arial are good examples of sans serif.

Serif Strokes on the arms, tails, and stems of letters. Serif text is often used to set large portions of text because the serifs help connect one character to the next and improve legibility. **Times Roman** is a good example of a serif font.

Uppercase THIS IS UPPERCASE. THE TEXT IS SET IN ALL CAPITAL LETTERS.

Upper- and Lowercase This is a combination of both upper and lowercase together.

Example: Lucy DeCillo and Ray Cogliano announce their wedding at Longwood Gardens.

X Height The height of the letters not including the ascenders and descenders.

For example:

See Spot run.

Downloading Templates *Quick tips to make you a techno-savvy crafter*

materials

~ computer

~ scanning program *(such as Photoshop)*

~ printer

~ paper *(see project instructions for appropriate kind)*

1. Log on to www.rockpub.com/100ideas and find the appropriate template.

2. Open your scanning program and then open the assigned template within the program.

3. Load your printer with some plain white paper. This will be your test paper. Print the template onto the paper and see how it looks. If the image appears too dark or too light, open the Image ➡ Adjustments ➡ Brightness/contrast menu. Move the arrow up or down to get an image that looks better to your eye.

This may vary according to your specific scanning program, so you may have to follow the software manufacturer's instruction manual to get the effect you want.

4. Load the paper tray with the paper needed for the project you wish to make.

5. Print out the template and follow the project's directions for trimming and folding.

Signed, Sealed, and Delivered

No letter is complete until it's in the envelope and stamped. The envelope is the first thing the recipient will see, so make your letter's debut smashing with these simple options.

Go Postal. Personalize your letters with PhotoStamps. Take your wedding photo, pet, or child's snapshot, or any other photograph that suits you, and send it to www.stamps.com. For about $16.99 per sheet of twenty, you can get your favorite image on the front of your letter.

Seal It, Stick It, Send It. Match the interior design with an outside sticker. For a flower card, use a matching flower sticker; for a funky dots card, use a simple colored dot. Retailers have a huge selection of stickers to match your mailing needs. Or, make your own custom version by placing a graphic on an adhesive-backed seal.

From Me to You. Make personalized return address labels to match your stationery. The Avery Label system works with Microsoft Word to help customize your labels. The Blank Template Library provides you with

a variety of templates to a label that coordinates with your envelope. Simply add your own text and graphics to a blank template. Clear labels are an especially nice option and work very well with a translucent vellum envelope.

Stamp It. Stamp the back of your letter with a coordinating rubber stamp. Or make a vegetable print or eraser stamp with your own design on it.

Tape This. A new line of decorative tapes is available at many stationery and art supply stores. Use these to seal an envelope flap. They come in a variety of widths and styles, including colored metallics and flowers.

Sealing Wax. A classic way of identifying yourself on an envelope is sealing wax. Press your initial into the sealing wax and send it out.

2 ›› Designing by Hand

Card of the Flies

This winged insect gets set in motion by using thread, a gift tag, and some good old-fashioned air.

materials

~ 8½" × 11"
   (22 × 28 cm)
   orange card stock
~ weave-patterned
   rubber stamp
~ fly rubber stamp
~ 4 red roundstone
   sequins
~ dark orange inkpad
~ dark green inkpad
~ 1" (3 cm) white tags
   with a metal frame
~ dark green thread
~ metal ruler
~ craft knife
~ scissors
~ cutting mat
~ 1¼" (3.5 cm)
   circle punch
~ drill punch
~ rotary trimmer
   with scallop-edge
   blade or scalloped-
   edged scissors
~ sewing needle
~ craft glue

Fits in a 5½" × 4¼"
(14 × 10.5 cm) envelope

1. Cut out a rectangle 5¼" × 7½" (13.5 × 19 cm) from the orange card stock.

2. Score then fold the card in half vertically so it measures 5¼" × 3¾" (13.5 × 10 cm).

3. Using the dark orange inkpad and weave-patterned rubber stamp, stamp the front of the card. You may want to test the stamp on a piece of scrap paper in order to get the technique down.

4. Let the ink dry for 10 minutes.

5. Mark the center of the card, then punch a 1¼" (3.5 cm) hole in the card with the circle punch.

6. Using the drill punch, make a small hole centered and about ⅛" (3 mm) above the large hole.

7. Using the dark green inkpad, stamp the fly on both the front and back of the metal tag and let it dry for about 10 minutes.

8. Meanwhile, cut the scalloped edges on three sides of your card with the rotary trimmer.

9. Sew the fly tag onto the card with the green thread, so it dangles in the center of the hole.

10. Glue four red roundstones into the corners.

VARIATION >> *If the weave-patterned rubber stamp is unavailable, try using real screening material from a hardware store.*

Spin Art Cards

Making these mini works of art at home instead of doing them at a carnival is great fun and makes splashy stationery.

1. Follow the directions on the spin art kit to make paintings and then let the spin art dry.

2. Trim the card down to 5" × 5" (13 × 13 cm) if the sheet is not already that size (the paper that comes with most spin art kits has a standard size of 5" × 5" [13 × 13 cm]).

3. Adhere the spin art painting to the front of a folded card.

materials

~ spin art kit complete with machine, paints, and 5" (13 cm) square sheets of card stock *(batteries required)*

~ 5½" (14 cm) square blue folded cards

~ glue stick

Fits in a 5¾" (15 cm) square envelope

ARTIST: ANNA HERRICK

TIP ➤➤ *For extra durability, flatten the cards under a heavy stack of books while the glue dries.*

Citrus and Sugar CD Cards

Don't burn a CD. Use it as a template instead! These tasty-looking fruit cards are a snap to make when you use technology as your guide.

materials

~ Citrus Fruit
  wrapping paper
~ CD
~ 8 ½" × 11"
  (22 × 28 cm)
  cream-colored
  card stock
~ Diamond Dust
~ craft glue
~ glue stick
~ craft knife
~ cutting mat

1. Place the CD directly over one of the fruit images on the wrapping paper and cut it out.

2. Fold the card stock in half. Place the CD on the card stock so that one side abuts the folded edge. Cut out, leaving a small portion of the card uncut at the fold for the hinge.

3. Glue the fruit image on to the cover of the card.

Place in orange or yellow 5" (13 cm) square CD envelope (Note: These envelopes only require standard postage.)

4. Make a circular glue line in the middle of the fruit and then make the glue lines radiate out from the center.

5. Sprinkle the glue lines with Diamond Dust and shake off the excess. Let dry about 1 hour.

TIP » *Use a box or a tray to contain the Diamond Dust debris.*

Cantaloupe- and Melon-Colored Paper Message Cards

Take advantage of the contrast between the soft green paper and the neon orange card stock to make these cards both elegant and happy.

1. Measure and cut out a 5¼" × 4" (13.5 × 10 cm) rectangle from the orange card stock.

2. Measure and cut out a 5¼" × 3¼" (13.5 × 8.5 cm) rectangle from the light green paper.

3. Draw a line ¼" (6 mm) from the long edge of the light green paper and score it with a craft knife and ruler.

4. Fold the paper on the score line and adhere it to the back of the orange card stock.

5. Starting ¾" (2 cm) in from the left and right sides of the light green paper, divide the space into five equal sections and mark the spaces with a pencil.

6. Using an alphabet punch set, create the word "HELLO," using the five sections to space out the letters.

7. Trim the bottoms of both the orange and green sheets with a decorative rotary trimmer or scalloped-edged scissors.

materials

~ 8½" × 11" (22 × 28 cm) neon orange card stock

~ light green decorative writing paper (Bachelor Button)

~ alphabet punch set

~ metal ruler

~ craft knife

~ cutting mat

~ glue stick

~ pencil

~ rotary trimmer with scallop-edge blade or scalloped-edged scissors

Fits in a 5½" × 4⅛" (14 × 10 cm) envelope

VARIATION >> *Create cards with other messages. Try "WELCOME," "CHEERS," or "CONGRATS."*

materials

~ square-tipped
  paintbrushes in a
  variety of widths
  (½"–1" [1-3 cm] widths)
~ blank watercolor cards
~ white acrylic gesso
~ watercolor dyes
  *(Dr. Ph. Martin or
  Luma Watercolor)*

Envelope sizes vary according
to each blank card set.

Mini Rothko

These easy-to-make cards are produced with washes
of watercolor dye and gesso.

1. Paint white gesso on the front of
   a blank card using any size brush.
   Make a circle, a square, a squiggle,
   or any shape of your choice with
   the paintbrush.

2. Let dry for an hour or so. It should be
   barely visible on the watercolor paper
   when dry.

3. Paint watercolor dye, either full
   strength or diluted with water, over
   the gessoed and ungessoed areas
   of the paper, again, creating a shape
   or pattern of your choice.

4. Apply a second ink color if desired.

ARTIST: ANNA HERRICK

TIP ›› *The ink that has absorbed into the untreated surfaces of the paper will have a dramatically different appearance
from the ink that dries on the surface of the gesso. The thickness of the gesso and density of the ink color can be varied
to create many different effects.*

Striped Gesso Cards

This vibrant variation of the mini Rothko cards
use bold colors and stripes to make a statement.

materials

~ paintbrushes with varied
  widths (½" – 1" [1–3 cm])

~ blank watercolor cards

~ white acrylic gesso

~ watercolor dyes (*Dr. Ph.
  Martin or Luma Watercolor*)

Envelope sizes vary according
to each blank card set.

1. The process for making these cards is
   the same as the mini Rothko cards
   described on the opposite page. The
   only difference is that stripes of gesso
   are painted horizontally across the
   card instead of in different shapes.

2. Once the gesso is dry, apply horizontal
   stripes of various ink watercolors.

3. Using a dry, rough brush to apply
   the gesso will make the brush strokes
   visible once the ink is applied. When
   applying a second or third layer of
   ink, you will get very different effects
   depending on the wetness of the
   previous layer. Use your imagination
   and have fun inventing your own
   techniques using these materials.

VARIATION >> *Experiment with different colors and shapes such as horizontal stripes,
polka dots, triangles or squares.*

materials

- ~ 1 large sheet decorative paper *(Forest Green Burst Rust Dot)*
- ~ 8 ½" × 11" (22 × 28 cm) cream-colored card stock
- ~ 5 ¾" (14.5 cm) square envelopes *(chartreuse)*
- ~ white oval acrylic jewels
- ~ ½" (1 cm) wide pink silk ribbon *(optional)*
- ~ cutting mat
- ~ metal ruler
- ~ craft knife
- ~ scissors
- ~ spray adhesive
- ~ bone folder
- ~ rotary trimmer with scallop-edge blade or scallop-edge scissors
- ~ hole punch *(optional)*
- ~ craft glue
- ~ envelope liner templates *(see optional step)*
- ~ glue stick

Fits in a 5 ¾" (15 cm) square envelope

Grandma's Wallpaper Gone Aglitter
Make these spectacular bursts even more beautiful with these little jewels.

1. Trim out a piece of the decorative paper to 5½" × 11" (14 × 28 cm), and use spray adhesive to adhere it to the sheet of cream-colored card stock. Use the bone folder to flatten the piece out.

2. Trim the card's edges with the scallop-edge scissors or a rotary trimmer.

3. Score and fold the card in half so the folded card measures 5½" (14 cm) square.

4. Each sheet of decorative paper has a repeating pattern of starbursts throughout the design. Adhere the acrylic jewels in the middle of each burst.

5. Punch a hole through all the layers on the bottom center of the card and run a 12" (30 cm) length of the pink ribbon through the holes. Tie the ribbon in a bow.

OPTIONAL STEP >> *Make an envelope liner to match your card. Trace and then cut out the liner using a 5 ¾" (15 cm) square envelope liner template. Trim the edges with the scalloped-edged scissors or rotary trimmer. Use the glue stick to adhere the liner to the inside of the envelope.*

Vamos a La Playa (Let's Go to the Beach) Stationery

These surfside beauties are a great way to correspond when you are down by the sea or just want to convey that summer feeling.

1. Cut a sheet of cream scroll paper down to 4¾" × 6¾" (12 × 17 cm).

2. Cut a 5" × 1" (13 × 3 cm) strip of wave paper, keeping the alignment of the waves horizontal. Give the top of the strip a wavy appearance by using a pair of scissors to cut along the top, following the shape of the waves. Adhere the strip to the bottom of the cream scroll sheet, leaving the excess hanging off the left and right sides of the sheet. Trim the strip flush with the edges of the cream scroll sheet.

3. Peel off a swimmer sticker and trim a little off the bottom of the feet or arms to make it look like that part of the body is already in the water. Place the swimmer on the second ripple from the top of the wave, about ¾" (2 cm) in from either the left- or right-hand side of the page (depending on what looks best to you).

4. Add a shell or a starfish sticker to the upper right- or left-hand corner about ½" (1 cm) in from the top and sides.

5. Add a sticker to the back of the envelope.

materials

~ 8½" × 11" (22 × 28 cm) cream scroll text
~ blue green wave paper
~ Victorian beach stickers
~ metal ruler
~ craft knife
~ scissors
~ cutting mat
~ glue stick

Fits flat in a 5¼" × 7¼" (13.5 × 18.5 cm) envelope

VARIATION » *If you cannot obtain this wavy paper, create your own with a pair of decorative-edged scissors.*

materials

~ 2 sheets of 6" × 8½"
  (15 × 22 cm) handmade
  watercolor paper in pink
~ white vellum
~ ⅜" (1 cm) wide brown
  ribbon with pink dots
~ bee stamp
~ dark green ink pad
~ spray adhesive
~ metal ruler
~ 1¼" (3.5 cm)
  circle punch
~ craft knife
~ cutting mat
~ glue stick
~ hot glue gun
~ rotary trimmer
  with scallop-edge
  or paper-edger scissors

Fits in a 5¾" × 8¾"
(15 × 22 cm) envelope

What's the Buzz? Stationery

Busy worker bees are spreading the news on this handmade sheet of paper.

1. Spray adhere the bottom two-thirds of two sheets of pink paper together.

2. Measure ¾" (2 cm) down from the top of the sheet and then punch out three circles (make sure you punch through both sheets of paper). Punch out the middle one first, making sure to center the circle on the page. Punch out the left and right circles, leaving about ½" (1 cm) in between each hole. You may want to test this out first on an ordinary sheet of white paper until you master the placement of the circles.

3. Cut out a 2" × 5½" (5 × 14 cm) strip of vellum and use the glue stick to adhere it to the back of the stationery, sandwiching the vellum between the two layers of pink paper. Note: Put the glue on the back of the watercolor paper, not the vellum.

4. Using the bee stamp and the dark green ink, stamp a bee in the center of each of the circular vellum windows.

5. Hot glue a 6¼" (15.5 cm) strip of ribbon across the page, approximately ¼" (6 mm) down from the three holes you previously made. Wrap and adhere the excess ribbon around the back of the first sheet of pink paper to the middle layer of the card.

6. Using the glue stick, adhere the back panel of pink paper to the back of the vellum layer.

7. Using the rotary trimmer with the scallop-edge attachment, cut the stationery down to 5½" × 7¾" (14 × 20 cm). This can also be achieved by using scallop-edged scissors.

Going Postal Stationery

Premade cards get a stamp of approval and some decorative paper coverings, which accentuate—not overpower—the dynamic architecture of the card.

1. Cut and then glue two strips of 2¾" × 5¾" (7 × 15 cm) Slab (pale green paint distressed) decorative paper to the front panels located under the triangular flaps of the card.

2. Trim the excess from the strips so they become flush with the card sides.

3. Adhere a coordinating stamp to the middle of the front triangular panels.

4. Place another stamp on the envelope flap.

5. Follow steps 1-4 using the other decorative paper and business envelope paper.

materials

~ pale green paint decorative paper (*Slab*)

~ blank cards with triangle flaps (*Beyond Postmarks*)

~ 1 sheet adhesive postage stamps for scrapbooking

~ natural decorative paper with lines

~ business envelope with blue-check patterned interior

~ glue stick

~ metal ruler

~ craft knife

~ cutting mat

Fits in a 4½"× 6" (11 × 15 cm) envelope

VARIATION >> *Use decorative-edged scissors on the triangular flaps to give them an antique look.*

materials

~ two 12" (30 cm) square sheets of water scrapbook background paper
~ #10 envelope
~ metal ruler
~ triangle
~ scissors
~ craft knife
~ cutting mat
~ tape
~ pencil
~ bone folder
~ glue stick

This project includes a #10 envelope, which you will make.

H₂O Stationery

Scrapbook making materials translate beautifully into stationery when pared down to the essentials.

1. Cut a sheet of the scrapbook paper down to 8 ½" × 11" (22 × 28 cm). This will be your letterhead.

2. Carefully open the seams of a #10 envelope and tape it on the back side of the scrapbook paper.

3. Trace the shape of the envelope onto the second sheet of scrapbook paper and then cut out the envelope shape.

4. Fold and score the edges of the new envelope with a bone folder and glue the sides of the envelope to the middle section (use the old envelope as your guide).

5. After you have written your message and placed it in the envelope, glue the top flap with the glue stick.

OPTIONAL STEP » *To personalize this stationery even more, typeset your name, address, and other pertinent information and print it out from your computer onto the letterhead.*

Rabbit Food Stationery

This macroversion of Mother Nature's finest grass makes you want to eat a salad—or maybe even a carrot.

For the folded grass card:

1. Cut a sheet of the grass paper down to 8" × 9 ½" (20 × 24 cm). Fold the card in half so it measures 4" × 9 ½" (10 × 24 cm). Score the edges with a bone folder.

For the rabbit card:

1. Cut a sheet of the grass paper down to 4" (10 cm) square.

2. Using a pencil, stencil a rabbit outline onto the back of the sheet.

3. Cut the rabbit shape out of the paper and glue the paper onto the card.

4. Punch a hole through both the card and grass paper layers for the eye of the rabbit.

5. Glue a strip of the felt ribbon next to the grass square and trim to the shape of the card.

For the envelope:

Follow the directions for the H$_2$O envelope on page 30.

materials

~ two 12" (30 cm) square sheets grass-background scrapbook paper
~ chartreuse felt ricrac ribbon
~ rabbit stencil
~ #10 envelope
~ tape
~ pencil
~ hole punch
~ glue stick
~ craft knife
~ cutting mat
~ metal ruler
~ triangle
~ bone folder
~ scissors

This project includes a #10 envelope, which you will make.

VARIATION » *Cut out, then glue, a felt carrot in the center of the ricrac ribbon.*

materials

- ~ 5¼" × 4½"
  (13.5 × 11.5 cm)
  A2 butter
  ricrac cards
- ~ five 2" (5 cm)-long flat
  flower pins in yellow,
  orange, and purple
- ~ ¾" × 4¾" (2 × 12 cm)
  lime green ribbon
- ~ 8½" × 11" (22 × 28 cm)
  orange card stock
- ~ metal ruler
- ~ pencil
- ~ double-stick tape
- ~ craft knife
- ~ cutting mat
- ~ glue stick

Fits in a #6
Baronial 5" × 6 ¼"
(13 × 15.5 cm)
envelope

Needles and Pins Notecard

Use straight pins and ribbon in an unconventional way to provide
a fresh, new way to look at spring.

1. Measure from left to right to determine the center point of the ricrac card. Once you have determined where the center is, measure 2¼" (5.5 cm) down from the top and mark that spot with a pencil.

2. Place your orange pin on that point and push it through to the back of the card. Then bring the point back out to the front of the card.

3. Add two additional pins on the left and right sides of the orange pin, placing a yellow and purple pin to the left and a purple and orange pin to the right. The pins are spaced roughly ⅝" (1.5 cm) apart. Vary the heights as shown.

4. Cut the ribbon strip to make fringes along one edge. Place double-stick tape on the back of the ribbon, then place the ribbon over the pin points about 1" (2.5 cm) from the bottom of the card.

5. Cut a 6" × 9½" (15 × 24 cm) rectangle from the orange card stock. Fold card stock in half vertically so it measures 6" × 4¾" (15 cm × 12 cm).

6. Center and then adhere the back of the ricrac card to the orange card stock.

ARTIST: CAROLYNN DECILLO

VARIATION » *Glue some embroidered flower patches on top of the flat flower pins for an even bolder statement.*

Bejeweled Leftovers

Combine vibrant silk-screened paper and rhinestones
to jazz up your old button and yarn scraps.

1. Cut out a 9" × 7" (23 × 18 cm) piece of the dotted paper.

2. Fold the paper in half so the card measures 4½" × 7" (11.5 × 18 cm).

3. Cut the upper and lower right-hand corners of the card with the rounded corner punch.

4. Draw a pencil mark centered horizontally and 2" (5 cm) from the top of the card. Make a 2" (5 cm) dot of glue with the pencil mark as the center.

5. Place one end of the orange yarn in the center of the glue circle and carefully wind a 2" (5 cm) diameter coil.

6. Adhere the buttons to the card, altering big and small buttons as shown in the photograph.

7. Dip the paintbrush in the glue and paint on some glue lines for the stems of the flowers.

8. To make stems, lay green yarn along the glue lines and then trim to the bottom of the card.

9. Glue the acrylic jewels into the center of each button flower.

materials

~ sheet of India text lime and yellow dot printed paper

~ assortment of pink and red buttons

~ scrap of orange yarn

~ scrap of dark green yarn

~ ¼" (6 mm) acrylic jewels

~ metal ruler

~ craft knife

~ cutting mat

~ rounded corner punch (Marvy)

~ pencil

~ craft glue

~ thin paintbrush

~ scissors

Fits in a 4½" × 7½" (11.5 × 19 cm) envelope

TIP >> *For an extra sturdy card, use spray adhesive to adhere the paper to card stock before folding and adhering all the ornamentation.*

materials

- corrugated cardboard cut down to 8" × 5½" (20 × 13 cm)
- ⅝" (1.5 cm) wide grosgrain ribbon
- stitched tin tiles *(Making Memories)*
- ¾" (2 cm) square scrapbook pebble
- dark green thread
- metal ruler
- bone folder
- scissors
- craft knife
- cutting mat
- computer *(optional)*
- layout software package *(optional)*
- craft glue
- 8½" × 11" (22 × 28 cm) white sticker paper
- sewing needle

Fits in a 4½" × 5¾" (11 × 15 cm) envelope

Shabby Chic Monogrammed Notecards

Classic typography paired with au naturel corrugated cardboard and a little grosgrain ribbon create a understated yet elegant environment for your words.

1. Fold the corrugated cardboard in half so it measures 4" × 5½" (10 × 14 cm) when folded. Press the edges of the fold with a bone folder for extra crispness.

2. Glue a 6" (15 cm) strip of grosgrain ribbon to the front of the folded card, aligning it vertically. Leave a little hanging off the top and bottom of the card. Trim the ribbon to the edges of the card and add a little glue to those same edges to prevent them from fraying.

3. Typeset the monogram for the card in white type on a ¾" (2 cm) black square. Print the monogram out on the sticker paper. If you don't wish to do this on a computer, you can use rub-down type or alphabet stamps printed with white ink on black paper.

4. Adhere the monogram to the tin tile and glue the metal plate about 1½" (4 cm) from the top of the card, centered on the ribbon.

5. Sew the corners of the metal plate and tie off the loose ends in a knot.

DIY Scrabble Card

Wordsmiths of the world unite. Scrabble supplies the scrapbook page. You supply the message.

1. Cut the maroon card stock down to 5 ½" × 11" (14 × 28 cm). Fold the card in half and score it with a bone folder. The folded card should measure 5 ½" (13 cm) square.

2. Cut the Scrabble scrapbook page down to 5 ⅜" (15 cm) square.

3. Spray adhere the scrapbook page onto the front of the card.

4. Compose your message on the board and attach the letters to the board using the adhesive dots.

materials

~ 12" (30 cm) square maroon card stock
~ Scrabble scrapbook sheet
~ Scrabble letters
~ ¼" (6 mm) double-stick adhesive dots
~ metal ruler
~ craft knife
~ cutting mat
~ spray adhesive

Fits in a 5 ⅛" × 3 ¾" (12.8 × 9.5 cm) envelope

TIP » *This makes a great gift as stationery. Make up several "board" cards and place them in a box with envelopes and a package of Scrabble letters for writing personalized messages.*

Clip It Good

It's Alexander Calder meets the office supply drawer. Pink paper clips are part form and part function when they hold colorful circles in place on your card.

1. Place a brown card on your cutting mat and mark the center of the card with a pencil. Using the lid as a template, cut around the outside of the circular shape with the craft knife.

2. Trim the edges of the card with the rotary trimmer or scallop-edged scissors.

3. Using the circle punch, cut out six circles of various colors from the scrap pack.

4. Slide the paper clips in and around the center hole and attach the colored circles to the ends of the paper clips.

5. Glue the brown card to the green card and place a pink rhinestone in the center.

materials

~ 5 ½" (14 cm) square brown card

~ 5 ½" (14 cm) square chartreuse card

~ scrap pack of card stock in shades of pink, orange, green, salmon, and cream

~ 5 pink paper clips

~ pink rhinestone

~ 1 ½" (4 cm) round lid, preferably metal

~ 1 ¼" (3.5 cm) circle punch

~ rotary paper trimmer with scallop-edge blade or scallop-edge scissors

~ cutting mat

~ metal ruler

~ triangle

~ craft knife

~ craft glue

~ glue stick

Fits in a 5 ¾" (15 cm) square envelope

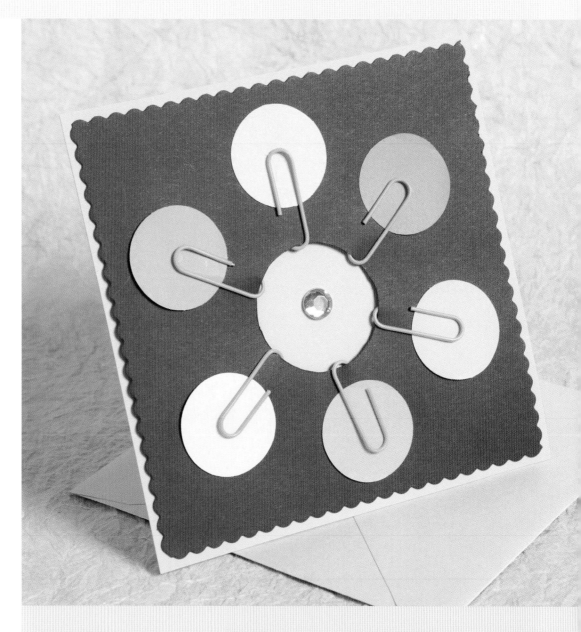

VARIATION >> *Place circular photos in the paper clips instead of the colored circles.*

Bagged and Tagged Stationery

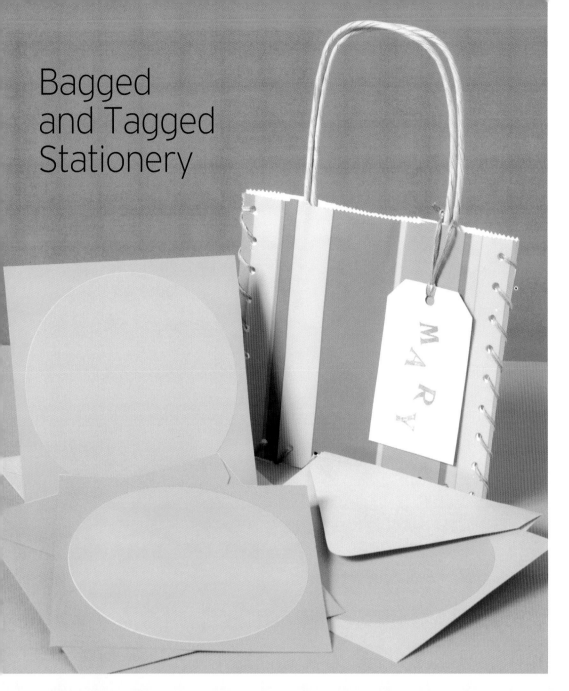

materials

- 5 ¼" (13.5 cm) square cards in jadeite, celery, and papaya
- 5" (13 cm) circle stickers in jadeite, celery, and papaya
- striped or decorative bag with handles
- grass green and celery green embroidery thread
- 4" (10 cm) light blue tag
- metal ruler
- cutting mat
- triangle
- hole punch or screw punch
- embroidery needle
- alphabet stamps
- orange inkpad
- green inkpad

Fits in a 5 ¾" (15 cm) square envelope

Customize a premade bag by cutting it down, sewing the edges, and adding the name tag of the recipient.

1. Adhere the stickers to the flat cards as follows: papaya sticker to the celery card; jadeite sticker to the papaya card; celery sticker to the jadeite card.

2. Cut the decorative bag down to 7" × 6 ¼" (18 × 15.5 cm).

3. Punch holes all the way around the outside edge of the bag, ¾" (2 cm) apart and ½" (1 cm) in from the edge of the bag.

4. Single thread a needle with three arm lengths of both the celery and grass colored embroidery threads.

5. Weave the thread through the holes around the edges of the bag and tie a knot at each end of the bag to secure.

6. Stamp the tag with the person's name, alternating between orange and green stamp pad. Tie the tag onto the bag with some of the remaining embroidery thread.

TIP >> *Use a sheet of lined paper placed on its side to get your holes equidistant from one another.*

ARTIST: CAROLYNN DECILLO

materials

~ 8 ½" × 11"
 (22 × 28 cm)
 pool blue fold-
 over cards

~ 1" (3 cm)
 silver-colored
 label holders

~ photographs
 from an i-Zone
 camera (or
 equivalent
 small prints)

~ metal ruler

~ craft knife

~ cutting mat

~ eyelet-setting
 tool

Fits in a 6 ¾" × 4 ¾"
(17 × 12 cm) envelope

Miniature Masterpieces

These postage stamp-sized photos are precious
to look at and make a lovely card.

1. Trim the pool blue card to 9" × 6 ¼"
    (23 × 15.5 cm).

2. Fold the card in half so the card
    measures 4 ½" × 6 ¼" (11 × 15.5 cm).

3. Place the label holders on the upper
    third of the front of the card and set
    the screws into place with the eyelet
    setting tool.

4. Trim to fit and slide prints into the
    label holders.

VARIATION >> *Use fancy label holders for more formal occasions such as weddings
and anniversaries.*

Heavy Metal Stationery Cards

Metallic card stock complete with typewriter keys and silver-colored eyelets make a modern, industrial statement.

1. Mark the center point of the silver cards, then score and fold them in half so they measure 4¼" × 5½" 10.5 × 14 cm).

2. Paste the red foldover cards into the interior of the silver cards.

3. Find the center point of the cover of the card and mark it with a pencil.

4. Align the edge of the hole punch to the right of the center point and make a hole. Repeat to the left of the center point so you have two holes total.

5. Center the typewriter keys in the holes and pierce the fasteners through to the back of the card. Hammer the fasteners to the card stock on the back.

6. Using the drill punch, make a hole through all the layers of the folded card about ½" (1 cm) from the left-hand side of the card and centered top to bottom.

7. Place an eyelet into the hole and flip the card open. Using the eyelet-setting tool and a hammer, set the eyelet in place. Repeat the same process on the back side of the card. Feed a 10" (25 cm) length of red ribbon through the hole and tie it in a bow.

8. Punch out the corners with rounded corner punch.

materials

~ 8½" × 5½" (22 × 14 cm) silver cards (*Stardream*)

~ 8½" × 5" (22 × 14 cm) red foldover cards

~ typewriter keys for scrapbook making (*Colorbök My Type Alphabet*)

~ silver-colored eyelets

~ ⅛" (3 mm) wide red ribbon

~ 6½" × 5" (15.5 × 13 cm) metal tin (*optional*)

~ pencil

~ metal ruler

~ craft knife

~ cutting mat

~ glue stick

~ ½" (1 cm) hole punch

~ hammer

~ drill punch

~ eyelet-setting tool

~ rounded corner punch

Fits in a 5⅝" × 4⅜" (A2) envelope

OPTIONAL STEP » *Place the cards in a 6½" × 5" (15.5 × 13 cm) metal tin. Puncture one of the typewriter keys in the center of a 2" (5 cm) circular tag. Punch four holes in the tag: top, bottom, left, and right; then run ribbon through the holes and tie in a bow on the bottom of the tin.*

materials

~ embossing foil

~ sheet of stiff felt

~ set of blank cards
  and envelopes

~ scissors or a
  craft knife

~ stylus tools or
  rounded lead pencil

~ circle template
  (optional)

~ glue stick

These premade cards
and envelopes come in
a variety of sizes

Foiled and Folded Cards

The 3-D effect of these embossed cards is both simple and elegant.

1. Cut out a 4" × 5¼" (10 × 13.5 cm) piece of embossing foil.

2. Place the colored side of the foil facedown on the stiff felt. (Whichever side of the foil you make an indentation on will cause the opposite side to protrude. You can certainly make indentations on either side of the foil.)

3. Use a stylus to draw a design, pattern, or image on the back of the foil.

4. If you would like more graphic elements, use plastic templates to trace circles or other shapes onto the foil. There are many decorative templates for embossing metal available in craft stores.

5. Once you are finished creating an embossed design, apply glue to the front of a folded card. Place the foil (colored side up) it on the card. Be careful not to press on the design you've created while doing this.

6. Trim off excess foil from the edges of the card.

ARTIST: ANNA HERRICK

TIP >> *The cards shown are decorated with gold foil, but there is a wide array of beautiful colored foil available at most craft stores.*

Streamline Photo Cards

A double-rounded corner card provides a stylish way to hold your favorite photos in place as well as a great place to write a message on the back.

1. Cut the silver card stock down to 5" × 7" (13 × 18 cm).

2. Cut the corners out with the double-rounded corner punch.

3. Glue one roundstone gem in each of the corners.

4. Place the photo in the frame, using the rounded corners to hold the photo in place.

materials

~ 8 ½" × 11"
(22 × 28 cm)
silver card stock
(Stardream)

~ 4" × 6"
(10 × 15 cm)
photo

~ 4 red
roundstone gems

~ metal ruler

~ craft knife

~ cutting mat

~ double-rounded
corner punch

~ craft glue

Fits in a 5 ¼" × 7 ½"
(13.5 × 19 cm) envelope

Parisian Postcard Stationery

Old becomes new when you use this antique Parisian postcard wrapping paper as the backdrop for your present-day letters.

For the stationery:

1. Cut out a piece of the wrapping paper to 6 ¾" × 9" (17 × 23 cm) and then trim all four edges with the rotary trimmer.

2. Cut a sheet of the blue vellum to 5 ¾" × 8" (15 × 20 cm).

3. Lay the blue vellum over the trimmed sheet of wrapping paper and center it.

4. Punch two holes in the top of the two sheets about 1" (3 cm) apart from one another and centered on the sheet on the right and left sides.

5. Cut a 12" (30 cm) length of the red ribbon and tie the two sheets together in a bow with the ribbon. Trim the ends of the ribbon on an angle.

For the envelope:

1. Carefully open the seams of a 7 ½" × 5 ½" (19 × 14 cm) envelope and tape to the back of a sheet of wrapping paper. Trace the outline of the envelope onto the back of the sheet of the wrapping paper with a pencil. This will be your template.

2. Remove the generic envelope and cut the envelope shape out of the wrapping paper using the craft knife.

3. Fold and glue the inside edges of the bottom outside panels, placing and adhering the bottom middle panel of the envelope on top of the other two panels.

4. Fold in the top panel of the envelope.

5. After you've completed your letter and are ready to seal, you can glue the top panel with the glue stick.

6. Wrap the envelopes up with some red ribbon.

7. Adhere the initials to the tag and tie it in to the bow.

materials

~ sheet of decorative Parisian postcard wrapping paper

~ 8 ½" × 11" (22 × 28 cm) light blue vellum

~ ⅛" (3 mm) wide roll of red satin ribbon

~ 1" × 2" (3 × 5 cm) red vellum tag

~ clear adhesive initials

~ 7 ½" × 5 ½" (19 × 14 cm) envelope

~ metal ruler

~ craft knife

~ cutting mat

~ rotary trimmer with deckled-edge attachment or decorative-edged scissors

~ hole punch

~ glue stick

~ bone folder

You will make a 7 ½" × 5 ½" (19 × 14 cm) custom envelope for this project

VARIATION >> *Using waterproof inks, personalize this stationery by handwriting the name of the recipient on the vellum tag.*

materials

- downloadable template: Initial Self Mailer petal template *(See page 18 for instructions.)*
- 8 ½" × 11" (22 × 28 cm) neon card stock in orange, and green
- ½" (1 cm) round adhesive hook-and-loop dots *(Velcro)*
- alphabet punch set
- metal ruler
- pencil
- craft knife
- cutting mat
- glue stick
- cellophane tape

Initial Self Mailers

These easy-to-make two-tone cards use neon card stock and the letter of your choice to pack a lot of punch.

1. Print and cut out the two pieces of the petal template.

2. Lay a piece of the orange card stock under the rectangular portion of the template. Trace around the shape, marking the fold lines on the card stock. Cut out the shape, then score and fold the card as marked.

3. Lay a piece of the green card stock under the rounded portion of the petal template. Trace around the shape, marking the fold lines on the card stock. Cut out the shape, then score and fold the card as marked.

4. Glue the rounded petal portion of the card to the back of the rectangular portion of the card, running the glue along the ¼" (6 mm) fold line.

5. Punch your initial in the center of the green flap. Then add a hook-and-loop adhesive dot to create a closeable flap.

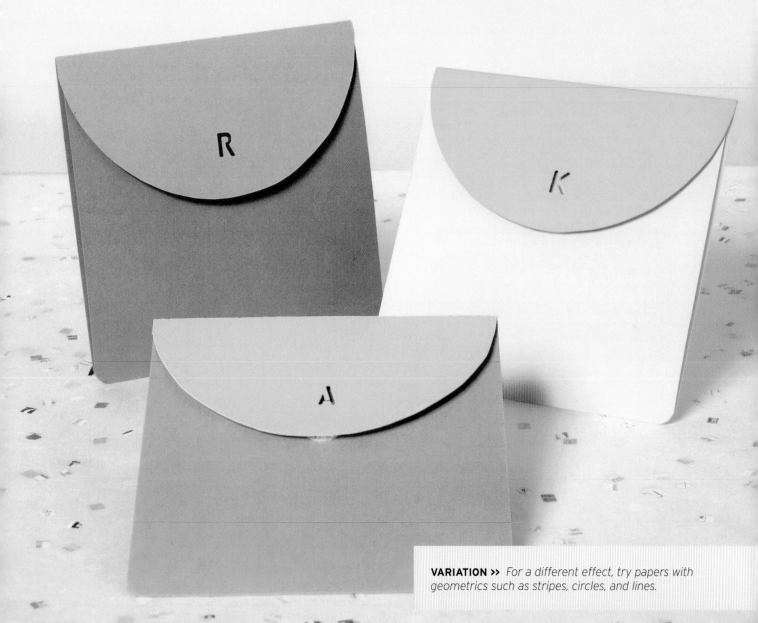

VARIATION >> *For a different effect, try papers with geometrics such as stripes, circles, and lines.*

Solid Gold Elvis Note Tags

materials

~ 5" × 2 ½" (13 × 6 cm) yellow gold note tags
~ Elvis stickers
~ 1" (3 cm) star punch
~ ⅛" (3 mm) wide gold ribbon
~ scissors
~ metal ruler
~ craft knife
~ cutting mat

Fits in a 3 ¾" × 5" (9.5 × 13 cm) envelope

From peanut butter and banana sandwiches to gold lamé, the King rocked our world. Continue the legacy by sending your words out on this perfect note.

1. Cut the note tag down to 4 ¾" (11.5 cm) wide.

2. Adhere an Elvis sticker to the left-hand side of the card, about ¼" (6 mm) from the eyelet.

3. Punch a star out of the lower-right hand corner, about ⅜" (1 cm) in from the side and bottom of the card.

4. Cut a 10" (25 cm) length of ribbon. Pull a loop of the ribbon through the eyelet, thread the two ends through the middle of the loop and pull tightly. Tie the ends in a knot and trim.

VARIATION >> *For more glitz, place a little gold glitter glue to the outside edges of the star.*

Tall Flower Stationery

 The rough edges of the watercolor paper and the hand stitching give this card its own anticommercial hallmark.

1. Cut a 9" 23 cm) length of ricrac ribbon and draw a 6 ¾" (17 cm) long stem on it with the marker.

2. Embroider the stem using a simple backstitch.

3. Hot glue the ricrac ribbon to the left- or right-hand side of the pink watercolor paper, about ½" (1 cm) in from the side of the paper.

4. Hot glue two leaves to the lower one-third of the stem.

5. Adhere the Petal Pebble to the top of the stem.

materials

~ 5" × 8 ½" (13 × 22 cm) sheet of handmade watercolor paper in pink

~ self adhesive Petal Pebbles

~ 1" (3 cm) wide lime green felt ricrac ribbon

~ olive green embroidery thread

~ embroidery needle

~ fine tip black marker

~ 1½" (4 cm) dark green leaf skeletons

~ hot glue gun

~ metal ruler

~ craft knife

~ cutting mat

Fits in a 5¾" × 8¾" (15 × 22 cm) envelope

VARIATION >> *The stem can also be hot glued instead of stitched, but the stitching gives it a more handmade look.*

materials

~ 8 ½" × 11" (22 × 28 cm) heavy maroon card stock
~ String Along kit
~ 5 ½" (14 cm) orange square card
~ tape
~ pencil
~ metal embroidery needle
~ metal ruler
~ craft knife
~ cutting mat
~ scissors
~ spray adhesive

Fits flat in a 5 ¾"
(15 cm) square envelope

String Has Strung Card

Math and needlecraft join forces to make this Spirograph-like card.

1. Center the velvet String Along board over the maroon card stock and tape it onto the card stock.

2. Trace the holes from the velvet String Along board onto the card stock and remove the tape. Set the board aside.

3. Thread the metal needle (do not use the one that comes with the String Along kit because you will need to pierce the card stock with it) with the yellow variegated embroidery thread and follow the directions for layer one in the kit, working your way in and out of the card stock to form the geometric sunset shape shown in the diagram that comes with the kit.

4. Cut the embroidered sheet of the maroon card stock down to 5½" (14 cm) square. Spray adhere it to the back of the orange square card.

VARIATION >> *Place a photograph or a sparkly gem in the center of the card for a little more glitz.*

materials

- 8 ½" × 11"
  (22 × 28 cm)
  neon card stock
  variety pack
- 2" (5 cm) alphabet
  stencil kit
- 4 ¼" × 5 ½"
  blank folded cards
  with envelopes
  (natural color)
- glue stick
- metal ruler
- triangle
- craft knife
- pencil
- cutting mat

Fits in a 4⅜" × 5¾"
(12 × 15 cm) envelope

Opposites Attract Notecards

The contrast between the dull brown card stock on the outside, and the bright
paper on the inside, makes reading this letter an inviting surprise.

1. Center the stencil on the front of the card and trace
   the initial. Open out the folded card and lay it face
   up on the cutting mat. Cut out the initial cap with the
   craft knife. Refold the card.

2. Cut out a 3½" × 4½" (9 × 11 cm) piece of the neon
   card stock and adhere it to the inner right side
   of the card, making sure to center it in the space.

VARIATION >> *Make the sheet on the inside 7" (18 cm) wide and glue it to the entire interior spread of the card.
This will give you more writing space.*

Odds 'n' Ends

This is a great way to use any scraps left behind from all the craft projects you've already done.

There are no steps. Take whatever you can find and decorate a card however you wish.

We've included several examples from which to take your cues.

materials

~ any size folded card and an envelope that it fits into

~ any papers, foil, or fabric

~ markers, paints, colored pencils

~ any other leftovers you find interesting

~ cutting mat

~ craft knife

~ scissors

~ glue stick

Start with the leftover envelopes you have and determine the size of the card based on the envelope size.

materials

~ downloadable template:
  Pat the Stationery *(See
  page 18 for instructions.)*
~ 1 large sheet
  decorative paper
  (Flock Fuchsia Dots)
~ 8 ½" × 11" (22 × 28 cm)
  maroon card stock
~ 8 ½" × 11" (22 × 28 cm)
  Chroma Lime vellum
~ 1 large sheet
  decorative paper
  *(Flock Fuchsia Wavy)
  (optional envelope)*
~ acrylic jewel
~ metal ruler
~ triangle
~ craft knife
~ cutting mat
~ spray adhesive
~ pencil
~ bone folder
~ craft glue

For this project you
can make a 6 ½" × 6"
(17 × 15 cm)
custom envelope

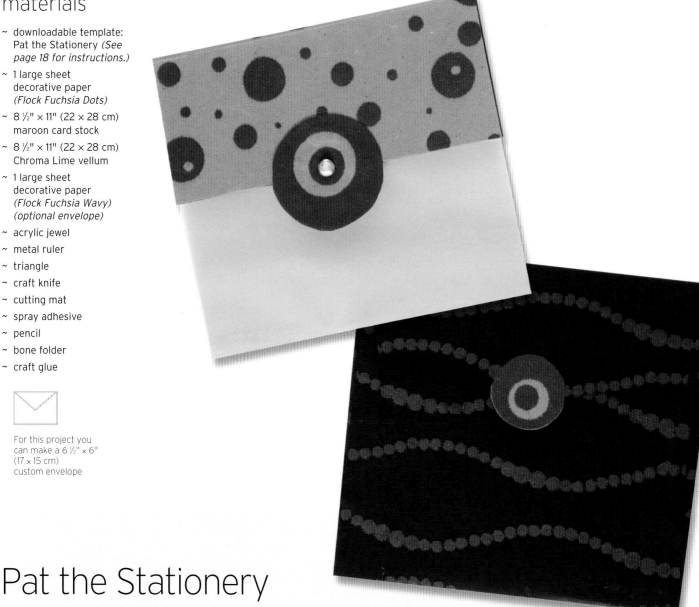

Pat the Stationery

Remember that '70s velvet wallpaper? Here it is in writing paper.
Who can resist rubbing the flocking on this not so distant cousin?

1. Cut out a sheet of dotted paper 6 ¼" x 8 ¼"
   (15.5 × 20.5 cm).

2. Cut out a sheet of maroon card stock 6 ¼" × 8 ¼" (15.5
   × 20.5 cm) and spray adhere the fuchsia dots paper to
   it. Make a pencil mark on the paper 2 ¾" (7 cm) from
   the top and fold and score the paper at that mark. Use
   a bone folder to make the fold line crisp.

3. Cut out a sheet of vellum 6 ¼" × 8 ¼" (15.5 × 20.5 cm).
   Make a pencil mark on the paper 3" (8 cm) from
   the bottom and fold and score the paper at that
   mark. Spray adhere the back of the remaining
   5 ½" (14 cm) of vellum to the bottom portion of the
   maroon card stock (see downloadable template).

4. Cut out then glue a large fuchsia dot to the front
   of the enclosure. Adhere an acrylic jewel to the
   center of the dot.

OPTIONAL STEP >> *Make a custom envelope from the wavy paper. Carefully open the seams of a 6 ½" × 6" (17 × 15 cm) envelope
and tape it on the back side of the decorative paper. Trace the shape of the envelope onto the decorative paper and cut out the
envelope shape. Fold and score the edges of the decorative envelope with a bone folder and glue the sides to the middle section
(use the old envelope as your guide). Cut the flap of the envelope along the wavy shape of the paper. Cut out and adhere a medium-
sized fuchsia dot to the flap and use it as a wafer seal.*

Get Flocked Letterhead

Sister stationery of Pat the Stationery

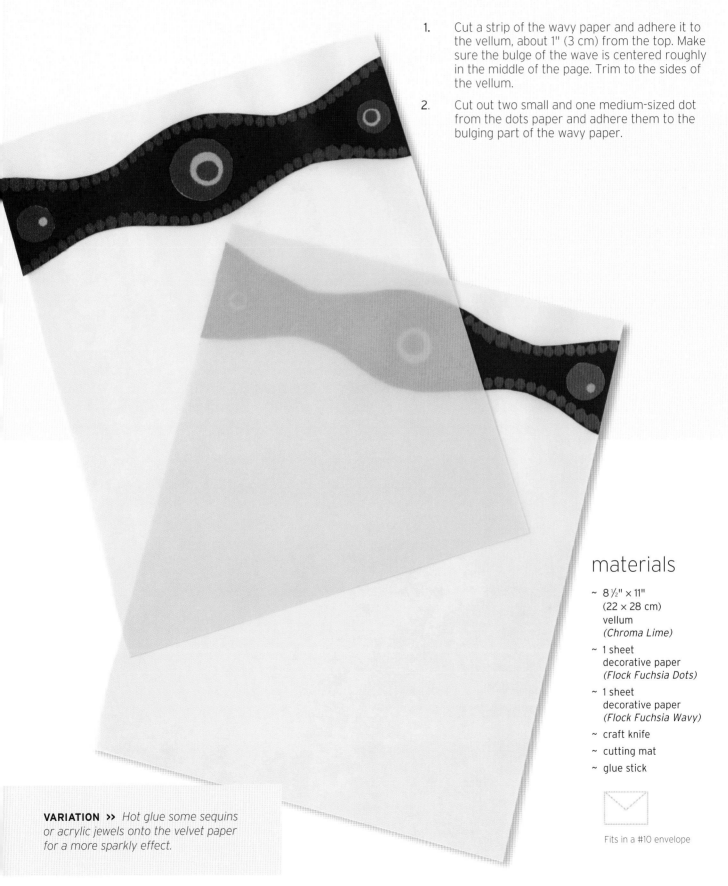

1. Cut a strip of the wavy paper and adhere it to the vellum, about 1" (3 cm) from the top. Make sure the bulge of the wave is centered roughly in the middle of the page. Trim to the sides of the vellum.

2. Cut out two small and one medium-sized dot from the dots paper and adhere them to the bulging part of the wavy paper.

materials

~ 8 ½" × 11"
(22 × 28 cm)
vellum
(Chroma Lime)

~ 1 sheet
decorative paper
(Flock Fuchsia Dots)

~ 1 sheet
decorative paper
(Flock Fuchsia Wavy)

~ craft knife

~ cutting mat

~ glue stick

Fits in a #10 envelope

VARIATION » *Hot glue some sequins or acrylic jewels onto the velvet paper for a more sparkly effect.*

materials

~ Eiffel Tower
  scrapbooking
  accent paper
  (Captured Elements)

~ chartreuse
  green card stock

~ 8 ½" × 11"
  (22 × 28 cm)
  white adhesive-
  backed paper

~ red photo corners

~ adhesive-backed
  letters

~ cutting mat

~ metal ruler

~ craft knife

~ bone folder

~ rotary trimmer
  with deckled-edge
  blade or deckled-
  edged scissors

~ color photocopier

Fits in a
#10 envelope

A Trifle Eiffel Card

Travel to Paris without actually going there
with these vertically magnificent cards.

1. Cut out a sheet of 7 ½" × 9" (17 × 23
    cm) chartreuse green card stock.

2. Score then fold the card stock in half
    so it measures 3 ¾" × 9" (10 × 23 cm).

3. Make a color photocopy of the Eiffel
    Tower image onto the adhesive-backed
    paper.

4. Trim the edges of the image with a
    deckled-edge blade or scissor, leaving
    about ⅛" (3 mm) for a white border.

5. Adhere the image to the card and place
    the photo corners on the edges.

6. Adhere the word "Paris" in an arc
    across the upper third of the image as
    shown in the photograph (right).

TIP ›› *These cards could make a fabulous theme package. Use a photo of the Tower of London,
with the word "London" written across it; the pyramids for Egypt, and so on.*

"Look Ma, It's Reversible!" Envelopes with Stationery

By covering both sides of this petal envelope with decorative paper,
you can decide on a whim whether to be playful or sophisticated.

For the envelope:

1. Brush some of the PVA glue on one side of the petal envelope and glue a sheet of the stitched paper onto the envelope.

2. Trim the excess paper with a craft knife using the edges of the petal envelope as your guide.

3. Repeat steps 1 and 2 on the flip side of the envelope, using the Indian text lime and yellow dot paper.

4. Fold the petals of the envelope in and press the edges with the bone folder.

5. Open out the petals and use a screw punch to bore a hole through two of the facing petals, approximately ³⁄₈" (2 cm) in from the outside edges.

6. Cut out two blue- and two lime-colored circles from the coordinating card stocks. Punch a hole in the centers of each with the ½" (1 cm) circle craft punch.

materials

~ 5 ¼" (13.5 cm)
   square chartreuse
   petal envelope

~ 1 sheet of stitched paper
   (Blue Green Stitch)

~ 1 sheet of India text lime
   and yellow dot paper

~ 8 ½" × 11" (22 × 28 cm)
   chartreuse vellum

~ blue card stock

~ lime card stock

~ PVA bookbinder's glue

~ bookbinding brush

~ metal ruler

~ craft knife

~ cutting mat

~ bone folder

~ screw punch

~ ½" (1 cm) circle
   craft punch

~ gold-colored
   scrapbooking screws

~ eyelet-setting tool

~ hammer

~ lime green
   embroidery thread

~ grasshopper
   rubber stamp

~ dark green inkpad

Fits in a #10 envelope

7. Align the blue circles with the holes on the petals on the blue sides of the paper and the lime circles on holes on the petals on the lime sides of the paper, placing a screw through each to hold them all together. Your layers should be as follows: blue circle, stitched paper, petal envelope layer, lime paper, lime circle and all should be held together with the screw.

8. Set the layers in place with an eyelet and eyelet-setting tool.

9. Wrap both sides of the enclosure with a piece of embroidery thread, twisting the thread underneath both of the blue cardboard circles on the blue side and the lime green circles on the lime side.

For the stationery:

1. Cut out a 5" (13 cm) square of the vellum and stamp a dark green grasshopper on the top center portion of the card.

OPTIONAL STEP FOR THE ENVELOPE >> *Cover the cardboard circles with the decorative paper for a more finished look.*

Monkey Business

Felt and ribbon make opening this birthday card a wonderfully tactile experience.

1. Cut out a 12" × 6" (30 × 15 cm) piece of the maroon card stock and fold in half so it measures 6" (15 cm) square.

2. Cut out a 6" (15 cm) square of pink felt and glue it to the front of the folded card.

3. Download the templates and print them out. Pin the templates to felt in the colors indicated on the template, and cut the shapes out with scissors.

4. Place and glue the monkey parts onto the front of the card in the following order: ears and top of head; face and jaw; mouth; nostrils; and party hat.

5. Glue a pair of ¼" (6 mm) googly eyes into the center of the white buttons and then glue the buttons to the face.

6. Cut a 13" (33 cm) long ribbon for the top of the card and a 20" (51 cm) long ribbon for the bottom of the card.

7. Fold the 13" (33 cm) ribbon in half and glue around the top front flap of the card. Leave the excess ribbon hanging off the right-hand side of the card. Tuck the excess ribbon between the felt and the card stock layer and glue it into place.

8. Fold the 20" (51 cm) ribbon in half and glue around the lower front flap of the card, leaving the excess at the right-hand edge.

9. Glue the pom-pom on top of the party hat.

10. Stamp the word "party" on a 2" (5 cm) orange circular tag with the green stamp ink.

11. Slip the tag onto to the bottom ribbon and tie the bottom ribbon in a bow.

12. Make an invitation on an 8 ½" × 11" (22 × 28 cm) document and trim it out to 5" (13 cm) square, insert and adhere it into the inside right interior panel of the card (not shown).

materials

~ downloadable template: Monkey Business (See page 18 for instructions.)
~ 12" (30 cm) square maroon card stock
~ 8 ½" × 11" (22 × 28 cm) pieces of pink, brown, maroon, and beige felt
~ ¼" (6 mm) googly eyes
~ two ¾" (2 cm) white buttons
~ 1 roll of ⅜" (1 cm)-wide orange and maroon scrapbooking ribbon
~ small bag of multi-colored pom-poms
~ 2" (5 cm)-wide circular orange and metal tag
~ metal ruler
~ craft knife
~ cutting mat
~ scissors
~ craft glue
~ rubber stamp alphabet
~ green stamp pad
~ straight pins
~ computer
~ printer

Fits in a 6 ½" (16.5 cm) square envelope

VARIATION >> *Pierce the monkey's ears and put in some beautiful earrings. Send it as a birthday gift card.*

Movers and Shakers Notecards

Who can resist the impulse to jiggle these cards back and forth?
Lenticular printed squares make these window cards come to life.

1. Center then adhere the image into the inside panel of
   the photo frame.

materials

~ red and sky 4-bar
  rounded photo
  frame cards

~ 1⅛" (3 cm) square
  lenticular printed image

~ craft glue

Fits in a 4-bar envelope

VARIATION >> *A miniature holographic image would also work well.*

materials

- ~ downloadable template: Pink Plastic Pachyderm *(See page 18 for instructions.)*
- ~ 8 ½" × 11" (22 × 28 cm) white printer paper
- ~ 1 sheet pink plastic gum
- ~ 8 ½" × 11" (22 × 28 cm) adhesive-backed labels
- ~ computer
- ~ scanning software *(Photoshop)*
- ~ metal ruler
- ~ craft knife
- ~ cutting mat
- ~ tape
- ~ screw punch
- ~ glue stick
- ~ bone folder
- ~ 6 ¼" × 9" (15.5 × 23 cm) envelope *(for optional step)*
- ~ decorative paper *(for optional step)*

Fits in a 6 ¼" × 9" (15.5 × 23 cm) envelope, directions below

Pink Plastic Pachyderm

Who says a card needs to be made out of paper? This rubbery plastic material makes a great notecard, invitation, or birthday card.

1. Download the pachyderm template and print onto the printer paper.

2. Cut out then tape a 10" × 6" (25 × 15 cm) piece of the pink plastic gum over the pachyderm template.

3. Cut out around entire the shape of the pachyderm (except for the eye), making sure to cut out the shape in and around the ear to define the elephant's face.

4. Use the screw punch to cut out the eye.

5. Adhere a sheet of the adhesive-backed labels onto the back of the pachyderm. Using the craft knife, cut out around the outside shape of the elephant. Write your note on the label side.

OPTIONAL STEP » *Carefully open the seams of a 6 ¼" × 9" (15.5 × 23 cm) envelope and tape it on the back side of the decorative paper. Trace the shape of the envelope onto the decorative paper and cut out the envelope shape. Fold and score the edges of the new envelope with a bone folder and glue the sides of the envelope to the middle section (use the old envelope as your guide). After you have written your message and placed it into the envelope, adhere the top flap with the glue stick.*

Go Ahead, Pull My Tongue Stationery

This card is inspired by my own very licky dog, Pluto, who, by the way, is a very good kisser.

1. Download the Dog Tongue template and print it onto an 8½" × 11" (22 × 28 cm) sheet of paper.

2. Tape the template page to the sheet of pink plastic gum and cut out the shape of the tongue with the craft knife. With the black marker, write in small type at the top of the tongue (just below the T shape), "Aren't you glad you just did that?"

3. Cut the blue sky background down to 8½" × 11" (22 × 28 cm) and spray adhere it to a sheet of white card stock. Cut out the dog head image and adhere it to the blue sky background, placing the dog head on the bottom of the page.

4. Cut a slit following the shape of the upper portion of the dog's mouth no wider than 1¾" (5 cm) wide.

5. Turn the card over so it is facedown. Slide the tongue into the slit of the dog's mouth, making sure the T bar is at the top. The T should prevent the tongue from pulling all the way out of the dog's mouth.

6. Turn the card face up and adhere a thought bubble sticker to the top of the dog's head. Write the words, "Go ahead, pull my tongue."

7. Turn the card face down again. Place double-stick tape on all four sides of the stationery and adhere it to another sheet of white card stock. Slide the tongue back into the dog's mouth and you are ready to send your note.

materials

- downloadable template: Dog Tongue (See page 18 for instructions.)
- 2 sheets 8½" × 11" (22 × 28 cm) white card stock
- piece of 8½" × 11" (22 × 28 cm) all-purpose paper
- sheet of pink plastic gum
- blue sky scrapbook background paper
- dog photo from a magazine
- computer
- scanning software

(Photoshop)
- metal ruler
- triangle
- craft knife
- cutting mat
- tape
- black fine point permanent marker
- thought bubble stickers
- double-sided tape
- glue stick

Fits in a 9" × 12" (23 × 30 cm) envelope

VARIATION » *This can work with just about any animal face. Photograph your own animal's face, scan it, and print it out onto some nice photo paper.*

Southwestern Tablecloth Cards

Nobody will be dusting crumbs off these lovely vintage fabric tablecloth cards.
A color copier can help you make multiple cards fast.

1. Cut a sheet of card stock down to 8½" × 5½"
    (22 x 14 cm). Score and fold it in half so it measures
    4¼" × 5½" (11 x 14 cm). Use a bone folder to make
    the fold crisp.

2. Color photocopy some sections from your tablecloth
    and trim the copies down to 3¾" × 5" (10 × 13 cm).

3. Glue the photocopy onto the front of the card.

4. Add glass beads, sequins, or other ornaments to
    enhance your image.

ARTIST: ANDY MCFADDEN

materials

~ various 8½" x 11"
  (22 x 28 cm) card stock
  in coordinating colors
~ vintage tablecloths
~ multicolored tiny glass
  beads or sequins
~ metal ruler
~ craft knife
~ cutting mat
~ bone folder
~ glue stick

Fits in a 4½" × 5¾"
(11 x 15 cm) envelope

VARIATION >> *Use a real tablecloth cut into sections and glue it onto the card with fabric glue.*

materials

~ downloadable template: El Rancho *(See page 18 for instructions.)*
~ 9½" × 11¾" (24 × 30 cm) recycled folder in natural brown
~ 8½" × 11" (22 × 28 cm) flannel paper
~ #2 pencil
~ linoleum block
~ linoleum block carving toolset with handle
~ 8½" × 11" (22 × 28 cm) sheet of Plexiglas
~ green, purple, and gold inks for block printing *(Speedo)*
~ brayer

Fits in a #10 envelope

El Rancho Stationery Set

Linoleum blocks are a great way to produce images over and over again. Once you've got it carved, you'll have it for many years to come.

1. Download the El Rancho template and print it out.

2. Place the template image side down on your work surface. Using the side of the pencil lead, rub the backside of the image to completely blacken it. Flip the template image side up, place it on top of the linoleum block and trace the outline of the image with a pencil, thereby transferring the pencil lead from the back of the paper to the linoleum.

3. Carve out the areas around the image with the linoleum carving set.

4. Place some green ink onto the Plexiglas and roll the brayer over the ink, going back and forth with the brayer until you hear a noise that sounds like Velcro ripping. Add a little stream of gold ink into the green on the Plexiglas and roll that gently with the brayer. Then roll the ink onto the image area of the linoleum block.

5. Press the linoleum block onto a white sheet of paper to test it to see how it looks. Once you've determined the carving looks good, stamp all over the outside of the folder, stamping at a variety of angles.

6. Once the ink has set up on the outside, open the folder and print some more on the inside flaps. (Shown in our version, purple ink on the inside.)

7. Stamp your individual sheets of speckled paper letterhead and envelopes with the linoleum block and ink.

TIP >> *The beauty of this technique lies in its rough-hewn appearance. Leave some edges higher and lower and see how you like the effect.*

ARTIST: JEANMARIE FIOCCHI-MARDEN

Native American Folded Feather Card

Materials found close to the earth, such as feathers, leather, and paper, are used to make up this natural looking stationery.

1. Paint the shaft of the feather with green craft paint using the fine brush. When dry, use the other end of the paintbrush dipped in turquoise craft paint to make some dots along the shaft of the feather.

2. Apply tacky glue to the portion of the shaft that has no feather veins attached. Wrap embroidery thread around the shaft in alternating colors. Be sure to tightly glue down the ends of the thread.

3. Tie a 12" (30 cm) piece of green thread around the feather where the shaft meets the veins, leaving 6" (15 cm) on each side. Embellish each end of the thread with a wooden bead and a turquoise bead. Separate out 1" (3 cm) of two individual threads of the embroidery thread. Put thread through the bead, and then tie a square knot to the other thread. Repeat on other side of tie.

4. Fold the 8 ½" x 11" (22 x 28 cm) terra-cotta card stock so it meets in the middle to form the card. Trim the turquoise card stock to 4 ½" x 7" (11 x 18 cm) using the pinking shears to get a zigzag design. Glue the turquoise paper inside the card.

5. Using the handle end of the paintbrush dipped in paint, make a dotted design on the front of the card with the red, turquoise, and green paints.

6. Glue the suede or felt to a scrap piece of card stock. Cut out a ½" (1 cm) diameter circle. Punch a hole for eyelet in the center. Apply the circles using an eyelet about ¾" (2 cm) from the center opening of the card, centered top to bottom.

7. Wrap the thread that is tied to the feather around the suede circles to hold card shut.

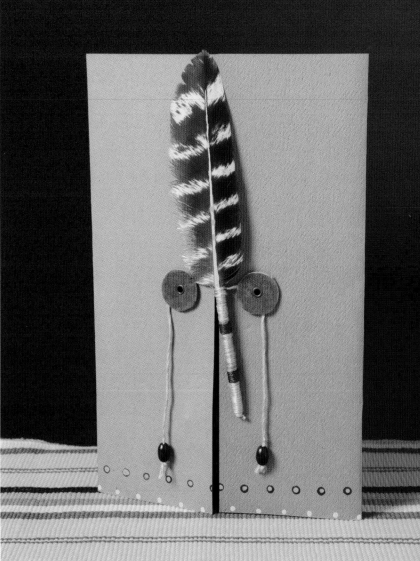

materials

- ~ 1 feather, approximately 7" (18 cm) long
- ~ 8 ½" x 11" (22 x 28 cm) terracotta card stock
- ~ 8 ½" x 11" (22 x 28 cm) turquoise card stock
- ~ craft paint in red, yellow, turquoise, and green
- ~ scraps of brown suede or felt
- ~ fine liner paintbrush
- ~ tacky glue
- ~ red, green, and turquoise embroidery thread

- ~ 2 medium-size wooden beads
- ~ 2 small turquoise beads
- ~ pinking shears or other decorative craft scissors
- ~ hole punch
- ~ eyelets and eyelet setting tool

Fits in a 5 ¾" x 8 ¾" (15 x 22 cm) envelope

TIP >> *Use a feather pen instead of a regular feather to make a really nice gift for someone.*

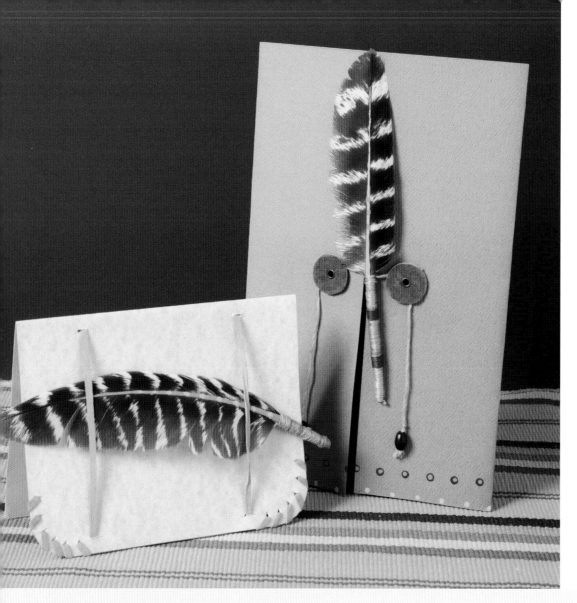

materials

~ downloadable template: Native American Notecard *(See page 18 for instructions.)*

~ 1 feather, approximately 6" (15 cm) long

~ 8 ½" × 5 ½" (22 × 14 cm) parchment card stock

~ fine liner paintbrush

~ craft paint in terra-cotta, green, and turquoise

~ tacky glue

~ terra-cotta, green, and turquoise embroidery thread

~ computer

~ printer

~ turquoise suede ribbon

~ craft knife

~ cutting mat

~ bone folder

Fits in a 4 ⅜" × 5 ¾" (12 × 15 cm) envelope

Feather Notecard

This variation of the Native American Folded Feather Card harkens back to the days when life was simpler.

1. Using the paintbrush, paint the shaft of the feather with turquoise craft paint. When dry, paint a design on the shaft with the green and terra-cotta paints; we used dots and arrows.

2. Apply tacky glue to the lower portion of the shaft that has no feather veins attached. Wrap embroidery thread around the shaft in alternating colors. Be sure to tightly glue down the ends of the thread.

3. Fold the 8½" × 5½" (22 × 14 cm) parchment card stock in half so it forms a card measuring 4¼" × 5½" (10.5 × 14 cm). Press the folder with the bone folder.

4. Download the feather template and print it out. Follow the template to trim the corners of card, and use craft knife to cut slits where indicated.

5. Thread ribbon through the slits in the card, using a whipstitch on the corners. Thread ends of ribbon under whipstitch on inside of card, and stick down with tacky glue.

6. Slide decorated feather under ribbon.

VARIATION » *Place a feather on a white sheet of paper and photocopy it for multiple pages.*

ARTIST: ANDY MCFADDEN

materials

~ cigar box
~ oversized sheet red
  and white clovers
  decorative paper
~ 5" × 7" (13 × 18 cm)
  cream-colored
  flat cards
~ 5¼" × 7¼"
  (13.5 × 18.5 cm)
  envelopes
~ metal ruler
~ craft knife
~ cutting mat
~ spray adhesive
~ bone folder
~ 3 pencils
~ gold initial
  wafer seals

Fits in an 5¼" × 7¼"
(13.5 × 18.5 cm) envelope

Smokin' Cigar Stationery Box

A great container since its inception: Grandma put her money in it under the mattress during the Depression. My brother stored his baseball cards in his. Why not fill a cigar box with some stunning personalized stationery, too?

1. Cut down a sheet of decorative paper to fit the length and width of your cigar box plus a little extra to cover the inside spine. Ours measures 7" × 7½" (18 × 19 cm). Spray adhere it to the inside of the box and smooth out the bumps with a bone folder.

2. Cut out a sheet of decorative paper to measure 8¼" × 5" (20.5 × 13 cm). On one of the short sides of the paper, cut around the shape of the clovers to form a scalloped edge. Spray adhere the decorative paper to the back of the flat card and wrap the remaining 1¼" (3.5 cm) flap around to the front of the card. The scalloped edge should be showing on the front of the card. Use the bone folder to smooth out any bumps.

3. Cut out a 1¼" × 11" (3.5 × 28 cm) band of the decorative paper and wrap it around the envelopes. Place a wafer seal on the band to finish it off.

4. From the decorative paper, cut out a piece 1" (3 cm) by the length of your pencils. Spray adhere the paper and wrap your pencils with it. Burnish it onto the pencil with the bone folder.

5. Place the pencils, some more wafer seals, and maybe some stamps in the box for a great gift.

VARIATION >> *Decorate the heck out of your box. Use beautiful paper, photos, or stamps to make it unique. Place a cigar box pocketbook handle and clasp on it for easy transport.*

Crimson and Clovers, Over and Over

An elegant pullout card housed in an enclosure is a sophisticated alternative to the standard envelope.

For the enclosure:

1. Download and open the Crimson Clovers template in your scanning package. Print it onto a legal size sheet of paper and cut it out.

2. Trace the template onto the red card stock.

3. Cut the red card stock out. Use the circle punch to make the hole in the area marked on the template. Then spray adhere a sheet of the decorative paper to the red card stock. Cut the decorative sheet of paper to match the red card stock's new shape.

4. Score and fold the card in the areas designated by the template. Fold the card in half and glue the edges in place.

5. Cut then glue a 15" (38 cm) length of ricrac around the card about 1" (3 cm) up from the bottom. Wrap it from the front to the back of the card leaving about ¼" (6 mm) on either end. Tuck the ¼" (6 mm) edges inside the enclosure and glue those into place.

For the card:

1. Cut out a piece of cream or red card stock 4 ¾" × 6 ½" (12 × 17 cm).

2. Cut and then spray adhere a 1" × 6¾" (3 × 17.5 cm) strip of decorative paper across the bottom of the card.

3. Using the craft glue, adhere a 6¾" (17.5 cm) strip of ricrac to the top of the decorative strip of paper and trim to the edges of the card. Add some craft glue along the edges of the ricrac to prevent it from fraying.

4. Place a typewriter key on the right-hand edge of the card, centering it top and bottom. Pierce the card with the prongs on the back of the typewriter keys and splay the edges with a screwdriver.

materials

~ Downloadable template: Crimson Clovers (See page 18 for instructions.)
~ oversized sheet red card stock
~ oversized sheet red and white clovers decorative paper
~ black ricrac ribbon
~ off-white card stock
~ typewriter keys for scrapbooks (Colorbök My Type Alphabet)
~ computer
~ scanning software (Photoshop)
~ legal size paper
~ pencil
~ metal ruler
~ craft knife
~ scissors
~ cutting mat
~ 1½" (4 cm) circle punch
~ spray adhesive
~ craft glue
~ screwdriver

Fits in an 5¼" × 7¼" (13.5 × 18.5 cm) envelope

materials

- 8 ½" × 11" (22 × 28 cm) neon card stock in orange and pink
- variety of coordinating decorative paper
- variety of pink and orange buttons
- adhesive-backed scrapbook initials
- metal ruler
- craft knife
- scissors
- cutting mat
- rounded corner punch
- sewing needle
- pink and orange thread
- orange embroidery thread
- glue stick

Fits in a 5" × 3 ¾" (13 × 10 cm) envelope

Personalized Button Stationery

Coordinated bright silk-screened paper and initialed button toggles are easy to craft and make a great gift.

1. Cut a 4¾" × 7" (12 × 18 cm) sheet of card stock.

2. Cut a 3½" × 7¼" (9 × 18.5 cm) sheet of decorative paper

3. Glue the decorative paper to the center of the card stock, leaving a little of the top and bottom of the decorative paper hanging over the edge.

4. Score and fold the card vertically so it measures 4¾" × 3½" (12 × 9 cm).

5. Trim the excess off the top and bottom of the decorative paper so it's flush with the card stock.

6. Punch out the rounded corners with the corner punch.

7. Sew a button to the front and back of the card about ½" (1 cm) in from the bottoms of each side of the card and centered.

8. Cut a 10" (25 cm) length of embroidery thread and wrap it around the back button first and then the front button.

9. Adhere an initial to the front of the button.

VARIATION >> *Instead of using an initial, adhere a very tiny photo of the person you are sending the letter to into the inset portion of the button. This can be achieved by either scanning the photo into your computer and scaling it down or reducing it on a photocopier.*

materials

~ one roll ¼" (6 mm)
  vintage bobbin ribbon
  *(yellow and orange
  checks)*

~ 4 ¼" × 5 ½" (10.5 × 14 cm)
  blossom-colored
  folded cards

~ chartreuse felt ribbon
  with ricrac edge

~ pink acrylic jewels

~ pencil

~ circle guide with
  2" (5 cm) hole

~ hole punch

~ scissors

~ craft knife

~ cutting mat

~ hot glue gun

~ white eraser

Fits in a 4½" × 6"
(11 × 15 cm) envelope

Taking a Ribbon Flower Card

This card was inspired by a flower I noticed on a shirt
belonging to Isabelle, my friend's 3-year-old daughter.

1. Using a pencil and the circle guide, draw a 2" (5 cm) circle 1" (3 cm) from the top of the folded card and centered on either side.

2. Find the center point within the 2" (5 cm) circle and divide the circle into eight equal segments, drawing lines from the center points to the edges of the circle.

3. Punch a hole in the center of the circle.

4. Lay the card out flat on the cutting mat and cut ¼" (6 mm) slits at the points on the outer edges of the circle. Erase the pencil marks.

5. Cut a 20" (51 cm) length of ribbon and feed it up through the center hole of the card, leaving a 1" (3 cm) tail inside the card.

6. Feed the ribbon in through any of the front slits, out through the inside front cover of the card, up through the center hole and in through the front of the next slit, and out through the inside front cover of the card. This will take the ribbon all the way around the circle.

7. Cut and then hot glue the ribbon onto the inside front cover.

8. Wrap a strip of ribbon around the bottom of the card from front to back and hot glue it. Trim the ribbon to the edges of the card.

9. Cut out a stem and some leaves from the felt ribbon. Hot glue them to the card.

10. Hot glue some embellishments here and there on the front of the card.

materials

~ flower and baby images
  cut out from magazines

~ 8" × 10" (20 × 25 cm)
  cardboard

~ assorted sticky
  letter type

~ white glue

Fits in a 9" × 12"
(23 × 30 cm) envelope

Lucy Arrives Birth Card

Changes in scale and the layering of magazine cutouts make this card one of a kind.

1. Arrange the flowers and laughing baby faces
    on the cardboard.

2. Glue images onto board with the tacky glue.

3. Place words on top of collaged materials
    (once they are dry).

VARIATION >> *Take your own digital photos of your baby and flowers and print them out onto*
photo paper and collage them together.

ARTIST: KATIE LIPSITT

Celebrate Mojo Birthday Card

The irregular edges, contrast of materials, and the lid from an old card box gives this card its own mojo.

1. Glue red sheer sparkle first followed by blue fringe material onto cardboard with craft glue.

2. Cut out the image of woman with mask with scalloped-edge scissors and glue onto the blue fringe fabric.

3. Stick letters and numbers on the card.

4. Glue a piece of manila envelope onto the back of the card and write your message there.

materials

~ assorted fabrics
  (red sheer sparkle and blue fringed)

~ 8" × 10" (20 × 25 cm) cardboard

~ card box lid image of woman with mask on

~ manila envelope

~ craft glue

~ scallop-edge scissors

~ assorted black-and-white sticky letter type

Fits in a 9" × 12" (23 × 30 cm) envelope

ARTIST: KATIE LIPSITT

Lucky Ladybug Card

Who can resist this pretty little insect hiding inside a four-leaf clover?

To assemble the ladybug:

1. Referring to the Lucky Ladybug template envelope section A, cut out:

   ~ the body out of red felt
   ~ the spots and feet out of black felt
   ~ the head out of gray felt
   ~ two round cheeks out of red mesh
   ~ flower petals from red felt
   ~ leaves and stems from green felt

2. Cut a 6" × 6" (15 × 15 cm) piece of sparkly green foam.

3. Remove the backing of the adhesive side of the ladybug's body and adhere it onto the square of green sparkly foam as shown on the template.

4. Adhere the black felt spots in positions shown on the template.

5. Use glue dots to place the cheeks on the head of gray felt.

6. Place a row of tiny adhesive red jewels to make the smile. (A mouth can also be made from a small piece of red felt or sewn on with red thread.)

7. To make eyelashes, cut eight short pieces, about ⅜" (2 cm) long, of thick black embroidery thread. Place a glue dot on the back of each googly eye and affix four eyelashes to it.

8. Once the face is assembled on the head, use glue dots to affix the head to the body.

9. Glue on and place the black feet as shown in the template.

10. Use the larger facetted red jewels to make centers for the flowers and arrange the red felt petals and green felt leaves and stems as shown.

materials

~ downloadable templates: Lucky Ladybug 1-3 (See page 18 for instructions.)
~ 1 sheet of bright green sparkly adhesive foam
~ adhesive sheets of pressed felt: red, black, gray, and green
~ clear adhesive dots small and medium
~ ¼" (6 mm) googly eyes
~ black embroidery thread or other thick black thread
~ tiny adhesive red faceted jewels
~ red facetted jewels about ¼" (6 mm) in diameter
~ large sheet of green card stock, at least 17" × 17" (43 × 43 cm)
~ light green paper
~ adhesive Velcro tabs
~ color mesh origami sheets (optional)
~ craft knife
~ scissors
~ glue stick
~ double-sided adhesive sheet

To make the clover-shaped envelope:

1. Refer to the Lucky Ladybug template envelope sections B, C, and D.

2. Transfer the pattern of the envelope onto the large sheet of green card stock.

3. Cut and assemble the pieces of the envelope.

4. Cut two half circles of dark adhesive green felt and two half circles of light green paper. Adhere them onto the flaps as shown in the template. Use a glue stick or double-sided adhesive sheet to paste the green paper half circles onto the flaps.

5. Using the shamrock pattern shown on the template, cut eight teardrop-shaped leaves out of the green sparkly foam and assemble them onto the dark green felt half circles as shown.

6. Cut a thin strip (no more than ¼" [6 mm] wide) of a double-sided adhesive sheet and use it to attach the bottom flap to the square panel.

7. Attach side flaps to the square section of the envelope.

8. Using the dull side of the craft knife, score the sections that will be bent.

9. Take the backing off of the 6" × 6" (15 × 15 cm) square of green sparkly foam with the ladybug on it and place it in the center of the square panel.

10. Gently bend the four flaps as shown.

11. Place one Velcro tab on the inside of the top flap and the other tab on the outside of the bottom flap, as shown on the envelope sections B, C, and D of the template.

12. Make one final flower (see envelope section A, back of template) with red felt and a red jewel center and affix it to the outside top flap.

TIP >> *A piece of pink mesh can be used in place of the red of the cheeks for the ladybug's mouth. You can also use felt for her mouth instead of the tiny red jewels.*

ARTIST: ANNA HERRICK

Oh Beehive! Card

Furry felt and fun foam make this card nice to touch and a refreshing break from paper cards.

materials

- ~ downloadable templates: Oh Beehive, Oh Beehive Card (See page 18 for instructions.)
- ~ 1 sheet of bright green sparkly adhesive foam
- ~ 1 adhesive sheet of stiff black felt
- ~ 1 adhesive sheet of stiff yellow felt
- ~ 1 adhesive sheet of stiff dark green felt
- ~ 1 adhesive sheet of stiff white felt
- ~ yellow glass micro marbles
- ~ ¼" (6 mm) googly eyes
- ~ yellow color mesh origami sheets
- ~ yellow and black thread
- ~ large sheet of yellow card stock 18" x 24" (46 x 61 cm)
- ~ white colored pencil
- ~ adhesive Velcro tabs
- ~ black thread
- ~ sewing needle
- ~ double-sided adhesive sheet
- ~ craft knife
- ~ scissors

ARTIST: ANNA HERRICK

For the bee art:

1. Refer to the Oh Beehive! template.

2. Cut a 6" (15 cm) square piece from a sheet of green sparkly foam. Do not peel the backing off the green foam until it is ready to be adhered to the interior of the card, which is the last step.

3. To make the center of the flower, cut a 3 ½" (9 cm) square from the yellow felt and double-sided adhesive. Remove the backing of one side of the double-sided adhesive and press it on top of the yellow felt. Do not peel the backing off the yellow felt at this point. Turn over and trace and cut out circle 1 from the yellow felt and adhesive.

4. Pour the yellow glass micro marbles in a small tray or dish (enough to cover a 3 ½" [9 cm] square area). Peel off the backing on the adhesive on circle 1 and press it into the pile of micro marbles. Set aside.

5. To make the flower petals, use circle 2 as a template to trace and cut out seven circles out of white felt.

6. Peel off the backing on the white felt petals. Arrange and stick them on the square of green foam, in the pattern shown in the template.

7. Cut the stem shape out of dark green felt and place it in the position shown on the template.

8. Peel off the backing on the yellow felt on circle 1. Place circle 1 (bead side up) in the center and partially cover the white petals.

9. To make the bee: trace and cut the bee's body out of yellow felt. Do not peel off the backing on the yellow felt at this point. Cut the black stripes out of black felt and stick on the bee as shown on the template.

10. Put a mini glue dot behind each googly eye and stick on the bee's face.

11. Using black thread, sew a smile on the bee's face.

12. Cut the wing shape out of yellow origami mesh. Fold in half. Using yellow thread, sew the wing onto the bee along the fold.

13. Peel off the backing on the back of the bee and stick on the flower.

For the striped card :

1. Please refer to the Oh Beehive! Card template.

2. Cut a 7 ½" x 16 ½" (19 x 42 cm) piece of yellow card stock.

3. Cut six black felt and five yellow felt strips 7 ½" x 1 ½" (19 x 4 cm). Do not remove the adhesive backing at this point.

4. Using a white pencil, trace a circle around an adhesive Velcro tab, onto the center of a black felt strip, as shown in template. Cut the circle out of black felt strip.

5. Peel off the backing on the black strip and place it flush left on the yellow paper with its edges perfectly aligned top and bottom.

6. Take the backing off the fuzzy half of the Velcro tab and embed it in the hole in the black strip.

7. Take the backing off the yellow strip and place it flush left against the right edge of the black strip. Continue to apply alternating black and yellow strips until the yellow paper is covered with vertical stripes.

8. Fold the card into three sections, along the fold lines on the template. Bend the folds so the yellow paper is on the inside and the striped felt panels are on the outside.

9. Place the "tooth" half of the Velcro tab on the yellow paper interior of the card. Make sure it is aligned with its fuzzy half before adhering to the yellow paper.

10. Peel off the backing on the green foam on the back of the bee art and place it in the center of second panel.

materials

~ downloadable template: Robo Card *(See page 18 for instructions.)*

~ 8 ½" x 11" (22 x 28 cm) white adhesive-backed paper

~ 6" x 9" (15 x 23 cm) silver sparkle adhesive-backed paper

~ 6" x 9" (15 x 23 cm) red sparkle adhesive-backed paper

~ 8 ½" x 11" (22 x 28 cm) metallic silver card stock

~ robot stickers *(optional)*

~ computer

~ color inkjet or laser printer

~ scanning software *(Photoshop)*

~ metal ruler

~ craft knife

~ cutting mat

~ drill punch

~ hole punch

~ rounded corner punch

~ double-stick foam mounting rectangles

Fits in an A2 envelope

Robo Card

Sparkle adhesive paper and metallic card stock give this little robot a techno-savvy look.

1. Download the robot template to your computer.

2. Print the robot onto an 8½" x 11" (22 x 28 cm) sheet of white adhesive-backed paper.

3. Adhere the robot template to the back of the silver sparkle adhesive-backed paper and cut it out with a craft knife and a straight-edged ruler.

4. With the drill punch, puncture three holes in each arm and leg following the holes on the template.

5. Cut out the black mouth and black TV shape from the template and adhere them to the front of the robot to match the photograph.

6. With the hole punch, punch out two circles from the red sparkle adhesive-backed paper for eyes. Adhere to the robot's face.

7. Cut out the arrow for the robot's stomach using the red sparkle adhesive-backed paper. Adhere the arrow to the center of the black TV screen as shown in the photograph.

8. Cut an 8" x 5½" (20 x 14 cm) rectangle from the metallic silver card stock. Fold in half to measure 4" x 5 ½" (10 x 14 cm).

9. Round the corners of the metallic card stock with the corner punch.

10. Cut a 3" x 4¾" (8 x 12 cm) rectangle out of the red sparkle adhesive-backed paper, round the corners with the corner punch, center the red paper over the folded metallic card, and adhere.

11. Place and adhere the robot to the card using the double-stick foam rectangles to add dimension.

VARIATION >> *Add robot stickers to the back of the envelope for a more cohesive package.*

Sculpey Swimmers

Showcase your clay creations on a greeting card.
This project is especially fun to do with kids.

1. On a clean, smooth surface, roll a ⅛" (3 mm) layer of polymer clay in any color you choose. Use a spatula to loosen the back of the clay to prevent it from being stuck to the work surface.

2. Use cookie cutters, a sharp knife, or modeling tools to cut out figures of people, animals, or any other shape. Your final clay shape should be no more than ¼" (6 mm) thick or it may not fit in the envelope once the card is finished.

3. Gently use your fingertip to smooth the cut edges of the clay shape.

4. Apply any texture to the surface of the clay, if desired.

5. Embellish the clay shape with molded pieces of clay in different colors. In the example shown, the fish scales are made by rolling a rope of clay in one color and then wrapping a layer of clay around it in another color. Take a sharp knife and slice the roll into thin circular sections, as if you were making tiny cookies. Press the circles to flatten them slightly and use them for decoration.

6. Once you are finished with your clay creation, carefully transfer it into an ovenproof glass dish and bake at 275° F (140°C or gas mark 1) for 15 minutes. Set aside to cool.

7. Apply glue to the back of decorative paper that complements the figurine you've made. Paste the paper on the front of a folded blank card. Trim off excess paper.

8. Once the baked shapes have cooled, place glue dots on the back of them and place them on the front of your card.

materials

~ blank folded card and envelope
~ polymer clay in various colors
~ decorative paper to complement clay
~ rolling pin
~ spatula
~ craft knife
~ cookie cutters or sharp knife
~ polymer clay modeling tools
~ glue stick
~ ovenproof glass dish
~ adhesive glue dots

Fits in a 4 ¾" x 6 ⅝" (6 x 17 cm) envelope

ARTIST: ANNA HERRICK

TIP » *Working with polymer clay offers infinite possibilities. This project features the use of individually colored polymer clays, but one can also purchase plain white clay and decorate it with acrylic paint after it has been baked. Many ideas and instructions for working with polymer clay can be found on Sculpey.com. There's also an endless array of tools and accessories for working with polymer clay that are available at almost any craft store.*

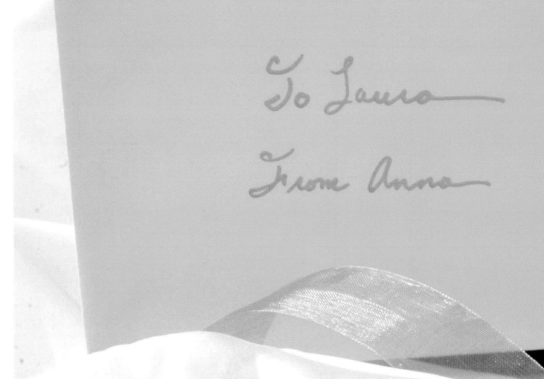

Flutter by Butterfly Card

This golden butterfly caught in mid air makes a whimsical notecard.

1. Refer to the Flutter by Butterfly templates.

2. Take an A2 size blue prefolded card or fold 8½" x 5½" (22 x 14 cm) piece of blue card stock in half to make a 4¼" x 5½" (10.5 x 14 cm) card. Using a gold metallic ink pen, copy the dot pattern shown on the template onto the front of the folded card. Set aside.

3. Use the template to cut out the two sets of wings, one out of gold foil and the other out of gold mesh. Please note that the gold mesh wings are not attached, but in two separate pieces.

4. Peel off the backing of a narrow strip of double-sided adhesive and stick it in the center of the gold foil wings (indicated by the red contour on the template) so that it covers the body area and slightly overlaps each wing. Trim off any adhesive beyond the edge of the gold foil wings.

5. Peel off the other backing on the double-sided adhesive. Adhere the inside edge of each gold mesh wing (the one facing the body) onto the adhesive on each gold foil wing. The adhesive in the body area should still be exposed.

6. Carefully place the glued wings into a shallow dish or tray. Pour yellow micro glass marbles over the exposed adhesive. Make sure the area is completely covered and gently press the marbles to secure them to the surface of the body. Gently shake the excess marbles off the wings.

7. Put glue dots in the positions shown on the template on the back of the foil

- ~ downloadable template: Flutter by Butterfly 1–2 *(See page 18 for further instructions.)*
- ~ A2 size blue prefolded card and envelope or 8 ½" x 5 ½" (22 x 14 cm) piece of blue card stock
- ~ fine point gold metallic ink pen 1.0 mm
- ~ gold embossing foil *(Amaco Art embossing foil)*
- ~ brass-colored wire mesh *(Paragona, 80-mesh woven)*
- ~ two 4 mm transparent yellow glass beads
- ~ two 2 mm transparent yellow glass beads
- ~ two head pins *(small pieces of wire used to make earrings)*
- ~ glass pebble
- ~ tiny adhesive facetted jewels
- ~ yellow glass micro marbles
- ~ double-sided adhesive sheet
- ~ ½" (3 cm) clear adhesive dots
- ~ invisible tape
- ~ craft knife
- ~ scissors

Fits in an A2 envelope

wings. Adhere the wings to the folded card as shown on the template.

8. To make the butterfly's head, apply tiny adhesive facetted jewels (in any color you choose) onto the curved side of a glass pebble to make two eyes and a smiling mouth. Set aside.

9. To make the antenna, take a 4mm glass bead and thread it through a head pin. Take the smaller beads and thread them through the head pin until there is a row of beads approximately 1" (3 cm) long. Bend to make a loop on the beaded end of the head pin. Repeat this step to make a second antenna.

10. Use a very small piece of tape to secure the exposed wire of the antenna on the folded card, above the body of the butterfly. Gently, but firmly, rub the tape until it's not visible on the surface of the paper.

11. Place a glue dot on the back of butterfly's head and stick it on top of the taped wires.

TIP >> *Write the recipient's name on the front in gold ink.*

TIP >> *The orange paper with gold leaf shown behind the bird is Joss paper. It is also referred to as Chinese spirit paper and can be found in some Asian shops. If it's not available in your area, the same effect can be created by gluing a piece of gold foil origami paper onto a piece of orange paper.*

ARTIST: ANNA HERRICK

78 100 IDEAS FOR STATIONERY, CARDS, AND INVITATIONS

Lovey Dove Card

The classic dove bearing the olive branch is a symbol of peace and holiday greetings.

materials

~ downloadable templates: Lovey Dove 1, Lovey Dove 2, Lovey Dove 3 *(See page 18 for instructions.)*

~ 7" x 10 ¼" (18 x 25.5 cm) yellow card stock or prefolded size A7 yellow card and envelope

~ gold leaf and orange Joss paper or orange paper and gold foil origami paper

~ gold embossing foil

~ brass-colored wire mesh

~ green foil origami paper

~ round gold sequin

~ small green cabochon

~ 1 sheet of thin cardboard

~ several clean sheets of all-purpose paper

~ a wooden block, cylindrical if possible

~ glue stick

~ double-sided adhesive sheet

~ ³⁄₁₆" (4.5 mm) and ½" (1 cm) clear adhesive dots

~ ¼" (6 mm) double-sided adhesive foam tabs

~ craft knife

~ scissors

Fits in an A7 envelope

1. Refer to Lovey Dove template.

2. Fold a 7" x 10 ¼" (18 x 25.5 cm) piece of yellow card stock in half to make a 7" x 5⅛" (18 x 13 cm) folded card. (If using prefolded cards, ignore this step.)

3. Using the glue stick, apply glue to the back of a piece of Joss paper and place it on the front of the card as shown on the template. Trim off the excess paper.

4. Trace the bird outline onto a sturdy piece of cardboard. See Lovey Dove 1.

5. Turn the cardboard over and apply a piece of double-sided adhesive to it.

6. Cut a 4½" x 3½" (11 x 9 cm) piece of gold embossing foil. Place it on top of a smooth surface (such as a pile of paper) and under a clean sheet of paper. Burnish it gently by rubbing a piece of wood over it. Toy wooden blocks, particularly cylindrical ones, work well for this.

7. Take the burnished piece of foil and place it on the adhesive side of the cardboard with the bird outline. Place a sheet of paper over the foil pasted on the cardboard and burnish it again.

8. Using a sharp pair of scissors, cut along the bird outline. Cut the slit shown on the beak.

9. Using the template of the wing, trace and cut the bird's wing out of the gold wire mesh. See Lovey Dove 2.

10. Place the gold wire mesh wing on the bird in the position shown in the template. Affix the wing to the body with a small, clear adhesive glue dot.

11. Trace and copy the outline of the branch onto a small piece of cardboard. See Lovey Dove 3.

12. Turn over and apply a piece of double-sided adhesive to it. Place a small piece of green foil origami paper to the adhesive side of the cardboard. Following the outline, cut out the branch.

13. Take the branch and insert it into the slit on the bird's beak as shown in photo. Secure the branch by placing a tiny glue dot between the top of the bird's beak and the obscured section of the branch.

14. Once the bird is fully assembled, place three double-sided adhesive foam tabs in the positions indicated on the template. Tip: Multiple stacked layers of double-sided adhesive foam tabs can be made to create a greater 3D effect of the bird against the background on the folded card.

15. Place the bird on top of the gold foil on the front of the folded card as shown on the top of template.

Floragami Card

Nature meets geometry when an origami enclosure is coupled with a lovely flower stamp.

1. From the full sheet of Cobalt paper, cut one piece 6" x 18" (15 x 46 cm). Mark and score 6" (15 cm) in from either end. Referring to the photo below, fold the left panel diagonally from upper left corner to lower right. Fold the right panel diagonally from upper right corner to lower left. Fold the left and right folded panels into the center panel left over right.

2. Punch a ⅛" (3 mm) hole through all layers in the bottom center of the card no more than ¼" (6 mm) up from the bottom. Tie the card with the narrow white ribbon.

3. From Iced Gold paper cut a piece 6" x 11" (15 x 28 cm). Fold the sheet in half so it measures 6" x 5 ½" (15 x 14 cm) folded. Punch a square out of the front of the folded panel, approximately ½" (1 cm) below the fold and centered. Adhere the solid panel to the back of the Cobalt card and fold the second panel with the punched square to the front of the card to make a flap. Tear ½" (1 cm) off of the bottom edge of the white flap.

4. Stamp your image several times with the Old Olive ink onto some Iced Gold paper. Let the ink dry thoroughly. Color with watercolor pencils and wet brush. Trim out your image and adhere it to a piece of 1 ¾" (5 cm) square Cobalt paper.

The unfolded card with the finished insert and the tag are shown here. Note the position of the diagonal folds on the cobalt panel.

ARTIST: MARY LAWLER

materials

- 1 sheet Canson Mi-Teintes #150 Cobalt 19" x 25" (48 x 64 cm)
- 2 sheets Canson Effects Iced Gold 8½" x 11" (22 x 28 cm)
- Canson Effects Iced Gold 6" x 6" (15 x 15 cm) envelope
- 12" (30 cm) narrow white satin ribbon
- 6" (15 cm) white decorative fiber
- Stampin' Up Close to Nature image
- metal ruler
- craft knife
- cutting mat
- ⅛" (3 mm) hole punch
- 1¼" (1.5 cm) square punch
- Stampin' Up Old Olive inkpad
- watercolor pencils
- paintbrush
- gold leafing foil
- glue pen
- small tag punch
- double-sided tape

Fits in a 6" (15 cm) square envelope

This is the card interior with the insert and tag in place.

5. With the glue pen, make four or five dots in the center of the flower and draw a rule line all around the square opening on the card's front. Let the glue dry for about 5 minutes. While the glue is still tacky, place gold leafing foil over the glued areas and rub lightly. When the foil is lifted the gold will remain where you put the glue.

6. Cut one piece of Cobalt 5¾" x 5½" (15 x 14.5 cm) and a piece of Iced Gold 5½" x 5¼" (14.5 x 13.5 cm) and adhere the Iced Gold paper to the Cobalt paper, centering it. Slide it into the main pocket of the card. Adhere the stamped image piece, from step 4, to the card so the image shows through the square window.

7. Punch out a small tag from some of the extra stamped images. Add white decorative fibers. Cut a 1¾" (5 cm) slit in the right diagonal fold pocket and slip the tag into the slit.

Finished project

VARIATION ›› *For a different look, try the same card with no window flap.*

materials

- ~ 60 lb light texture watercolor paper
- ~ paper towel (a smooth surface with no printed pattern is best)
- ~ assorted fresh picked botanicals (pansies, violas, violet leaves, blue phlox, creeping phlox, verbena, ferns, Japanese maple leaves, cosmos, scaevola, and dill)
- ~ mulberry paper (optional)
- ~ metal ruler
- ~ craft knife
- ~ cutting mat
- ~ smooth cutting board
- ~ hammer

Fits in an A6 envelope

Pounded Botanical Stationery

The physically satisfying art of pounding flowers and other botanical materials with a hammer to transfer their pigment to another surface is a wonderful technique.

1. Cut paper to 6 ¼" × 9" (15.5 × 23 cm). If the paper has a deckle edge, plan to use that at the top or bottom of the stationery for a handmade look.

2. Layer two sheets of paper towel on the cutting board, and place a sheet of trimmed paper on top. Arrange fresh, dry botanicals in a pleasing pattern on the paper. You may need to separate and reassemble petals if the flower centers are too thick to hammer well, and you'll have best results if you pinch off all stem and leaves from the flower base.

3. Cover the flowers carefully with another sheet of paper towel. Begin to hammer the flowers through the paper until you can see the pigment bleed through the top paper towel. Make certain that you hammer all the edges of the flower, and that you've had direct contact with all of the flowers' interiors.

4. Lift off the paper towel, and remove the flower and leaf remains. Let dry.

VARIATION >> *Glue small, facetted, flat-bottomed body gems to your stationery for sparkle and glamour.*

materials

- ~ library pocket *(Boxer)*
- ~ patterned paper *(Captured Elements)*
- ~ library card *(Boxer)*
- ~ packing tape
- ~ stencils
- ~ blue spray paint
- ~ number rub-ons *(Jeneva & Co.)*
- ~ date stamp
- ~ inkpad
- ~ book text
- ~ clear rubber bands

The pocket will fit inside a standard size envelope; however, any envelope could be created to accommodate the size of the pocket.

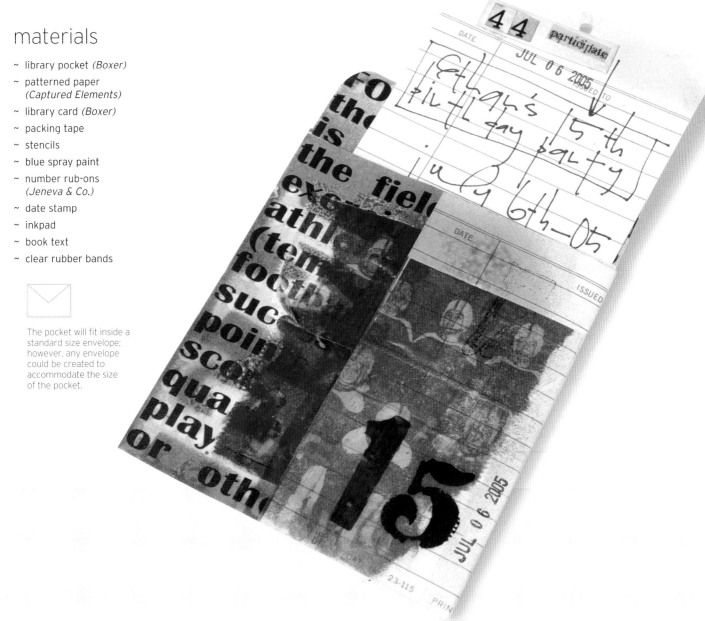

Overdue for a Birthday Celebration

This artful rendition of a library card in its pocket will remind people a party is coming soon.

1. To embellish the pocket, transfer the image from the patterned paper onto the packing tape. Place a piece of packing tape over the top of the image you want to transfer. Take away excess paper, and put the taped piece in warm water for 2-4 minutes. Remove from water and roll the paper from the tape. The image will transfer onto the packing tape. There should still be some adhesive left on the tape; therefore, I usually use the adhesive as well. The tape transfer works great as a dimensional piece.

2. Use the stencils and some spray paint to place the initials on the side of the pocket.

3. Place rub-on letters for age on the front of the library pocket.

4. Stamp the date of the birthday on the front of the pocket as well.

5. Embellish the library card with book text.

6. Punch a hole in the top of the library card and loop a clear rubber band through the hole.

7. Write the party information by hand.

Shipping Tag Cards

A series of unique tag cards can be made by folding large shipping tags in a matchbox shape. Once the tags are embellished, hold them together with a jeweled pin.

1. Stain shipping tags with walnut ink.

2. Fold the shipping tag like a matchbook; fold the bottom upwards approximately halfway, then fold top down so that it barely overlaps the bottom flap.

3. Staple the top fold in in place, so it mimics a real matchbook cover.

4. Embellish the outside of the tags with image transfers from patterned paper rub-ons.

5. Open the tag and punch two holes in the bottom fold. Size a piece of library record paper to fit inside the tag, punch holes to line up with the holes in the bottom fold, and with floss, tie the paper inside the tag. When all tags are embellished, group the tag cards and hold together but running the pin through all the holes, and secure clasp.

materials

~ large shipping tags
~ walnut ink
  (Anima Designs)
~ patterned paper
  rub-ons
~ library record paper
~ foam stamp
~ acrylic paint
~ stapler and staples
~ hole punch
~ ribbon
~ floss
~ vintage jewel pin

Fits in a 5" square (13 cm)
square padded envelope

TIP » *Use an acrylic paint color to match the rhinestones on your pin.*

ARTIST: STEPHANIE MCATEE

Tree of Life Birth Announcement

What better symbol for announcing a growing, young baby? A linoleum block is a great way to give a rough-hewn, natural look to your announcement.

1. Open the Tree of Life Tree template, print it out, and rub all over the reverse side of the printout with a pencil. Use the side of the pencil to cover the entire area to be transferred. Cut the drawing out and tape it face up on a 3¾" × 5" (10 × 13 cm) linoleum plate.

2. Using a good amount of pressure, trace over the lines of the drawing with a pencil so they transfer onto the linoleum plate. Remove the drawing and darken any lines with the pencil where needed.

3. Insert a size 3 cutter into the linoleum cutting handle.

4. Heat the iron on the cotton setting, no steam. Place a sheet of copier paper above and below the plate and heat the linoleum by ironing it (an ironing board is a fine surface for this procedure). Note: You may have to heat the plate several times while you are carving. Heat the plate whenever carving becomes difficult.

5. Using the carving tool, carve out the areas that will not receive ink. While carving, remember to cut away from yourself.

materials

~ downloadable templates: Tree of Life Tree, Tree of Life Sun, Tree of Life Flower *(See page 18 for instructions.)*

~ printing paper or colored copy paper

~ paper for card *(Canson)*

~ colored paper for mounting print

~ wallet-sized child's photo

~ scissors

~ #2 pencil

~ template

~ linoleum block 3¾" × 5" (10 × 13 cm) plates

~ linoleum cutters, size 3

~ cutting handle

~ iron/ironing board

~ copier paper

~ water-based printing inks *(in two colors)*

~ brayer

~ paper plate

~ glue stick

~ colored pencil

~ metal ruler

~ craft knife

~ cutting mat

~ computer

~ printer

~ scanning software *(Photoshop)*

Fits in an 6 ¼" × 4½" (15.5 × 11 cm) envelope

6. Squeeze out 2" (5 cm) lines of orange and yellow printing inks side by side on your paper plate. Roll the brayer up and down and side to side in the orange and the same with the yellow, then back to the orange. The inks will randomly mix. You are ready to ink the plate when you hear a noise that sounds like Velcro ripping while rolling the brayer in the inks. This noise indicates good coverage on the roller.

7. Roll the brayer over the linoleum plate. Move the brayer up and down and side to side, covering the entire plate.

8. Carefully pick up the plate with your index fingers and place, ink side down, on a clean piece of colored printing paper. Press on the back of the plate, making sure there's good contact between the plate and the paper.

9. Cut out prints leaving about ⅜" (2 cm) around all sides. The prints will measure approximately 4" × 5⁷⁄₁₆" (10 × 14 cm).

10. Repeat steps 1-9 with the Tree of Life Sun template and Tree of Life Flower template.

11. Mount each print on another piece of paper, 5⁵⁄₁₆" × 5⁷⁄₈" (13.5 × 15 cm), leaving more space on the bottom so you can write your message. I used blue papers, blue for the print and blue for the frame. This gives the card more depth and provides space for the lettering. When mounting, use a glue stick and cover the entire back of the print.

13. Cut out a photo of your child. Using a glue stick, glue the photo in the center of the flower print.

14. Cut the card from the Canson paper with the textured side down, 13¾" × 6¼" (35 × 15.5 cm). Hold the card horizontally and fold the right edge of the paper in 4½" (11 cm). This is the short fold. Fold the left edge of the card to meet the edge of the right side.

15. Glue the mounted tree print on the front of the card. Open the card and glue the mounted sun print on the second fold. Reserve the flower print for later.

16. Using the colored pencil, write "OUR TREE IS BIGGER" below the tree print in block letters. Repeat steps 11-15 for the additional mounted prints. "OUR DAYS ARE SWEETER (OR SUNNIER)" for the sun print and "HOW WE LOVE OUR BABY BOY/GIRL" under the flower print.

17. Cut an additional panel from this mounting paper 4⁵⁄₁₆" × 5⁷⁄₈" (10.5 × 15 cm). This will be for the announcement panel. Handwrite your baby's stats in block letters. Glue this announcement panel to the center inside panel of the card.

18. Place the mounted flower print/photo insert on top of this panel. This is a loose panel that does not get glued.

EXTRA ENVELOPE DETAILS » *Cut a detail (I used the sun) from any of the extra prints you might have and glue onto the back flap. Another spot for a small detail (maybe a swirl) is the top upper left-hand corner on the front of the envelope. Write the return address next to the design.*

ARTIST: JEANMARIE FIOCCHI-MARDEN

Leathery and Lovely
Mini Stationery Portfolio

This book is bound for glory. Learn simple bookbinding techniques or just make the cards inside.

materials

~ downloadable templates: Leathery and Lovely template, Leathery and Lovely figures *(See page 18 for instructions.)*

~ white card stock

~ large sheet of decorative paper *(Camden Fair "Beads on Chartreuse")*

~ turquoise vellum (Chromatica)

~ 13" × 19" (33 × 48 cm) sheet of book board

~ 9" × 12" (23 × 30 cm) piece of rawhide leather

~ 3" × 1" (8 × 3 cm) metal label holder

~ thin cardboard

~ metal ruler

~ utility knife

~ craft knife

~ cutting mat

~ scissors

~ spray adhesive

~ bone folder

~ tape

~ glue stick

~ leather glue

~ 1" (3 cm) sponge brush

~ upholstery hammer

See project directions
for the custom envelope

For the stationery:

1. Cut out a 7½" × 5¾" (19 × 15 cm) piece of white card stock.

2. Cut out a 7½" × 5¾" (19 × 15 cm) piece of decorative paper. Spray adhere the decorative paper onto the white card stock and smooth out any bumps with the bone folder. Lightly score then fold the card in half so the folded card measures 3¾" × 5¾" (10 × 15 cm). Make five cards using this method.

For the envelope:

1. Open and print out the Leathery and Lovely template.

2. Cut the template out and tape it onto a sheet of the vellum. Trace around the shape and cut the envelope out using a pair of scissors.

3. Score the edges of the envelope with a bone folder and glue flap A to flap B. Use a little glue stick on the underside of flap A to bond A and B together. Glue flap C to A and B, again using a little glue stick on the underside of the flap.

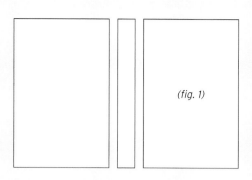

(fig. 1)

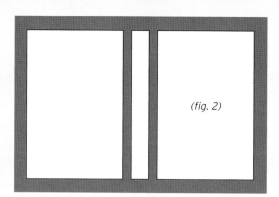

(fig. 2)

1. Cut two pieces of book board each 4½" × 6" (11 × 15 cm). These will be your front and back covers. For the spine, cut a ½" × 6" (1 × 15 cm) piece of book board *(see fig. 1)*.

2. Lay the piece of leather facedown on your work surface. Coat the book board and leather surfaces with the leather glue and center the book board on the leather, leaving about ⅛" (3 mm) between the spine and the front and back covers *(see fig. 2)*.

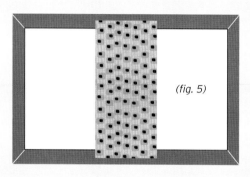

(fig. 5)

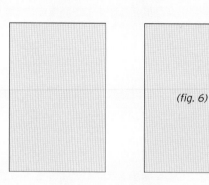

(fig. 6)

4. Cut a 3" × 6¼" (8 × 15.5 cm) sheet of decorative paper. Center it on the spine and adhere it to the spine and adjacent areas *(see fig. 5)*.

5. Cut two new boards from the thin cardboard 4⅜" × 6¼" (11 × 15.5 cm) *(see fig. 6)*.

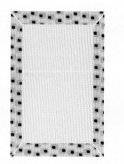
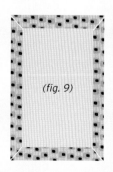

(fig. 9)

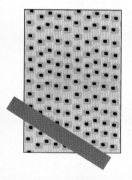
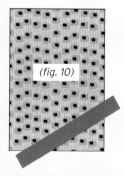

(fig. 10)

8. Burnish the paper onto the cardboard, making sure to get out all the air bubbles *(see fig. 9)*.

9. Cut two 1" × 6" (3 × 15 cm) strips of leather and place them on a diagonal over the decorative side of the boards, one starting about 3¼" (8.5 cm) down the left-hand side of the board and the other starting the same distance on the right-hand side of the board *(see fig. 10)*.

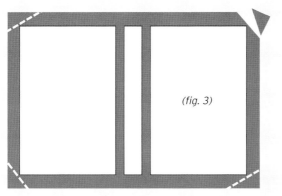

(fig. 3)

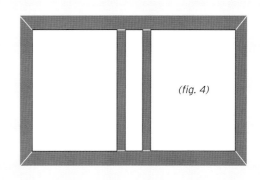

(fig. 4)

3. Cut the corners of the leather on a diagonal so they can be mitered later *(see fig. 3)*. Place some more glue the overhanging edges of leather and fold the edges inward onto the boards *(see fig. 4)*. Try to make the mitered edges of the leather be flush with one another and not overlap. Burnish the leather with the bone folder and push the leather into the spaces between the spine and covers to form a crease.

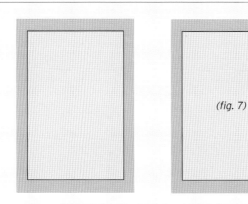

(fig. 7)

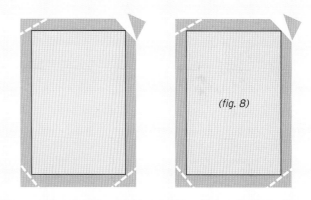

(fig. 8)

6. Cut two sheets of decorative paper 5 ½" × 7 ½" (14 × 19 cm). Place the new sheets facedown on the work surface. Adhere the newly made boards to the plain side of the decorative paper, making sure to center them on the decorative paper *(see fig. 7)*. Keep in mind these will be two completely separate boards.

7. Cut the corners on a diagonal, add some more glue to the overhanging edges and fold the edges to the back side of the boards *(see fig. 8)*.

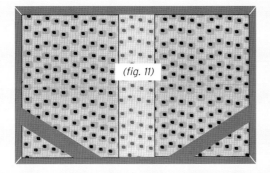

(fig. 11)

11. Nail and glue the label holder to the front cover of the book and make a label from the leftover blue vellum. You can place a plain white sheet of paper behind the vellum to make the name really pop. If you don't own a computer, use rub down type or alphabet stamps to make the typography.

10. Glue the overhanging parts of the leather to the back side of the thin cardboard panels. Glue the composited panels with the leather diagonals to the inside front and inside back panels that you made in steps 1–3, placing the glue on the back sides of the leather diagonal panels *(see fig. 11)*.

Flower Power Notecard and Box

This pretty box filled with a set of notecards and matching envelopes makes a lovely gift.

For the flower notecards:

1. Download and print out the Flower Power 1 template. Take a 5 ½" × 11" (14 × 28 cm) piece of blue card stock and fold it in half to make a 5½" (14 cm) square folded card or use prefolded 5½" (14 cm) square cards.

2. Trace the flower shape onto a piece of pink paper and cut out.

3. Using the glue stick, paste the pink flower centered to the front of the card.

4. Using the petal templates, cut out a total of eight petals from the origami mesh—four red and four magenta.

5. Take the four red petals and place them on the pink flower, in the positions shown on the template. Affix the bottoms of the petals to the pink flower with clear adhesive glue dots.

6. Using the template for circle 1, cut a circle out of teal-colored paper. Place a glue dot on the back of it and place it in the center of the card, partially covering the bottoms of the red mesh petals.

7. Take the four magenta petals and place them, in the positions shown on the template, on top of the teal circle. Affix the bottoms of the petals to the pink flower with glue dots.

8. Using the template for circle 2, cut a circle out of dark teal-colored paper. Place a glue dot on the back of it, and place it in the center of the card, partially covering the bottoms of the magenta mesh petals.

9. Using the template for circle 3, cut a circle out of the hot pink iridescent paper. Place a glue dot on the back of it, and place it in the center of circle 2.

10. Use a 5¾" (15 cm) square blue envelope to accompany the finished card.

For the flower notecard box:

1. Download and refer to the Flower Notecard Box template.

2. Using the glue stick, apply a layer of glue to the back of the hot pink iridescent paper.

3. Cover the sides and top of the lid of the box with hot pink iridescent paper. The paper does not have to cover the whole area of the top, but should cover ½" (1 cm) along the edge. Tuck paper under the rim of the box and secure with a small piece of double-sided adhesive.

4. Cover the sides and the inside rim of the bottom with pink paper. Glue and secure paper in the same manner as steps 1 and 2.

5. To make the small flowers that decorate the sides of the box, place a mini glue dot on the back of a pink facetted jewel and stick on top of a white spoke sequin.

6. Place a mini glue dot on the back of a white facetted jewel and stick on a silver spoke sequin.

7. Make ten flowers of each type, for a total of twenty flowers.

8. Each side of the box will have a row of five alternating flowers. Using mini glue dots, adhere the flowers to side of the box as shown in photo.

9. To make the flower decoration on the top of the box, apply glue on a 5¾" (15 cm) square piece of paper and place it in the center of the top of the lid.

10. Using the Flower Power template, cut five petals out of pink tissue paper and five petals out of magenta origami mesh. Adhere to the top of the box using a glue stick.

ARTIST: ANNA HERRICK

for the card

~ downloadable template: Flower Power (See page 18 for instructions.)

~ 5 ½" × 11" (14 × 28 cm) blue card stock or blue pre-folded 5½" (14 cm) square card

~ 5¾" (15 cm) square envelope

~ hot pink irridescent paper

~ red and magenta origami mesh

~ pink paper

~ small piece of teal-colored paper

~ small piece of darker teal-colored paper

~ ½" (30 cm) clear adhesive dots

~ glue stick

~ craft knife

~ scissors

for the box

~ downloadable template: Flower Notecard Box (See page 18 for instructions.)

~ square box with lid that can fit 5¾" (15 cm) square envelopes inside of it

~ pink paper

~ hot pink iridescent paper

~ Ten ¼" (6 mm) round pink facetted jewels

~ Ten ¼" (6 mm) round white facetted jewels

~ 10 white spoke sequins

~ 10 silver spoke sequins

~ magenta origami mesh

~ pink tissue paper

~ small piece of thin cardboard

~ metal ruler

~ craft knife

~ scissors

~ cutting mat

~ double-sided adhesive sheet

~ mini clear adhesive glue dots

~ glue stick

materials

- ~ downloadable template: Bride Card (*See page 18 for instructions.*)
- ~ 5 ½" (14 cm) square superfine white folded card
- ~ 5 ½" (14 cm) square flat card (*Stardream Quartz*)
- ~ 5 ¾" (15 cm) square (*Stardream Quartz*) envelope
- ~ craft embossing silver foil
- ~ white satin fabric
- ~ white origami mesh

- ~ 1 sheet of thin cardboard
- ~ 1 ½" (3.5 cm) wooden domed disc
- ~ 5 mm artificial pearl beads
- ~ white thread and needle or thin wire
- ~ metal ruler
- ~ craft knife
- ~ scissors
- ~ cutting mat

- ~ double-sided adhesive sheet
- ~ several clean sheets of all-purpose paper
- ~ white paint
- ~ wooden block, cylindrical if possible
- ~ ½" (1 cm) clear adhesive dots
- ~ transparent glass micro marbles
- ~ glue stick

Bride's Card Revisited

A sparkling flower of satin and white mesh on pearly paper makes a lovely card to accompany a wedding gift.

1. Download Bride Card template.

2. To make satin petals: Peel one side of a 9½" × 2¾" (24 × 7 cm) piece of double-sided adhesive to a piece of silver craft embossing foil. Do not remove the backing of the other side of the adhesive at this point.

3. Take a 9½" × 2¾" (24 × 7 cm) piece of white satin, iron if necessary. Remove the backing of the adhesive on foil. Carefully, lay the satin on the adhesive. Be mindful not to get any bumps or air bubbles between the satin and the foil.

4. Using the petal template and a pair of scissors, gently trace and cut out five white satin petals.

5. Put a petal between two clean sheets of paper, foil side up. Using a smooth wooden block, gently burnish the petal from top to bottom. This will cause the satin side of the petal to curve outward. Burnish the four remaining petals.

6. Put a glue dot on the narrow end of the foil side of each petal. Place the petals in a circle on the folded card, in the positions shown on the template.

7. Using the petal template, cut five petals out of white mesh.

8. Place the white mesh petals in the spaces between the white satin petals as shown on the template. Adhere to the card with glue dots.

9. To make the center of the flower, take a small piece of cardboard (2" [5 cm] square) and the 1½" (3.5 cm) wooden domed disc and paint them white.

10. When the paint on the cardboard is dry, apply one side of a double-sided adhesive to it. Do not remove the backing of the other side of the adhesive at this point. Turn it over and trace and cut out circle 1. Set cardboard circle aside.

11. When the paint on the wooden domed disk is dry, apply one side of a double-sided adhesive to it. Do not remove the backing of the other side of the adhesive at this point.

12. Pour transparent glass micro marbles into a small dish. Peel off the backing of the adhesive on the domed disc. Press the adhesive into the glass micro marbles.

13. Peel off the backing of the adhesive on the cardboard circle. Carefully center the domed disk on top of the cardboard circle, marble side up, so there is a narrow rim of exposed adhesive on the cardboard circle.

14. Make a string of small pearls, using either thin wire or a needle and white thread.

15. Carefully wrap the string of pearls around the domed disk. The pearls will adhere to the exposed adhesive on the cardboard circle below it.

16. Once the center is completed, place glue dots on the back of the cardboard and place it in the center of the petals.

17. Use a 5 ¾" (15 cm) square stardream quartz envelope to accompany card.

materials

- ~ downloadable template:
  See Spots Run *(See page 18 for instructions.)*
- ~ large sheet of bookbinding cloth
- ~ 3 large sheets of rice paper *(yellow with a printed white pattern, a soft white sheet with black and wax dots, and an oversized irregular black polka dot)*
- ~ letterhead stock in muted yellow
- ~ #10 gray envelopes
- ~ coordinating ribbon
- ~ metal ruler
- ~ craft knife
- ~ cutting mat
- ~ spray adhesive
- ~ chipboard cut to the size of the pockets
- ~ bone folder
- ~ double-sided tape

Use #10 envelopes
inside the portfolio

ARTIST: MARY KREINDEL

See Spots Run Stationery Folio

Soft, natural colors and textures offset with strongly contrasted ink blots remind us of Dalmatians and Jackson Pollack.

1. Trace the edges of the See Spots portfolio template on the back side of the large sheet of bookbinding cloth.

2. Cut slits for ribbons.

3. Use spray adhesive to paste decorative rice papers to the bookbinding cloth inside and out as you want them to appear once folded and glued. Use clean paper to mask out areas that will not receive adhesive and to prevent overhanging paper to not stick where you don't want it.

4. Cut out the folder using the paper template you used to trace the shape onto the bookbinding cloth.

5. Score folds lightly with a craft knife on the inside of the folds. Using a straight, clean piece of chipboard close to the thickness of your pocket depth, fold the portfolio along each score and form pockets around the board. Use the bone folder to make clean, crisp folds.

6. Adhere pocket flaps with double-sided tape.

7. Insert the ribbon into the slits on the inside back the folder.

8. Insert letterhead and envelopes into the folder and tie the ribbon in a bow in the front.

3 >> Hybrid Designs

Using Both the Computer and Handmade Techniques

Favorite Flake

Kirigami, along with some shiny embellishments and vibrant colors, make this holiday card shine.

1. Follow the directions for making Kirigami flowers on page 11 of the paper folding kit (examples 2-4 from the kit are shown in the photo).

2. Spray adhere the finished flowers onto the square cards as follows: purple flower on jadeite card, pink flower on celery card, and lime green flower on blue card.

3. Paint a thin layer craft glue under the page pebbles and place the button over your photo. Cut the photo out around the shape of the button and glue the button into the center of the Kirigami flower.

4. Glue the acrylic jewels around the outer edges of the petals.

materials

~ 5 ⅕" (13.5 cm) square cards in jadeite, blue, and celery

~ Kirigami paper folding and cutting kit *(Unfold the Secrets of Kirigami)*

~ ¾" (2 cm) page pebbles

~ 1" (3 cm) photos or copies of photos

~ variety of acrylic jewels

~ spray adhesive

~ craft glue

~ craft knife

~ scissors

~ cutting mat

~ paintbrush

~ hot glue gun

~ computer *(optional)*

~ word processing program *(optional)*

~ printer *(optional)*

Fits in a 5 ¾" (15 cm) square envelope

OPTIONAL STEP » *Either handwrite, stamp, or typeset the words "Happy Holidays from Your Favorite Flake" on the back of the square card.*

materials

~ downloadable template: Instant Messaging Calligraphic Ornament *(See page 18 for instructions.)*

~ 8" × 10" × 2 ½" (20 × 25 × 6 cm) chartreuse photo box *(Kolo)*

~ 8 ½" × 11" (22 × 28 cm) orange card stock

~ decorative paper *(Tiles on Violet)*

~ white adhesive-backed inkjet or laser paper

~ page layout software

~ metal ruler

~ craft knife

~ calligraphic ornament template

~ glue stick

~ novelty "pencil pen" *(optional)*

Fits in a 4 ½" × 7 ½" (11 × 19 cm) envelope

Instant Messaging
Index Card Gift Set

Send off a quick note with these colorful, personalized index cards.

1. In your page layout program, create a new 8½" × 11" (22 × 28 cm) document.

2. Create a 7" × 4" (18 × 10 cm) rectangle and center it in the document.

3. Download and import Instant Messaging Calligraphic Ornament.

4. Set your initials in 15-point Baskerville semibold in lowercase, place it in a maroon circle, and make the type white. Position it in the center of your calligraphic ornament.

5. Set your name in 8-point Baskerville semibold.

6. Create nine maroon dotted lines under the name, 24 points apart and alternating between 6 ¼" (15.5 cm) wide and 6 ½" (17 cm) wide on every other line.

7. Print cards out on the orange card stock.

8. Cut out and glue a sheet of 7⅜" × 9⅝" (19 × 24.5 cm) decorative paper to the inside of the box lid.

9. Replace the Kolo insert in the front window of the box with a piece of the decorative paper.

10. Create a 24-point initial cap M or letter of your choice and place in a ½" (1 cm) maroon circle. Print it out on the white adhesive-backed paper, trim the circle, and place it in the center of the patterned paper in the window.

11. In your layout program, copy the card one time and paste it under the first card, and center both cards on the page so the cards can be stacked two-up for printing.

materials

~ 12" (30 cm) square
  sheet of light green
  paint-textured paper
~ 6" × 9" (15 × 23 cm)
  sheet of Asian
  Joss paper

~ 6" × 9" (15 × 23 cm)
  green corrugated
  cardboard
~ turtle rubber stamp
~ computer

~ word processing
  or page layout
  program (MS Word
  or Quark XPress)
~ color printer
~ rotary trimmer with
  scallop-edged blade or
  scallop-edged scissors

~ metal ruler
~ craft knife
~ scissors
~ cutting mat
~ copper-colored
  inkpad

~ glue stick
~ 4 burnt orange eyelets
~ screw punch
~ eyelet-setting tool
~ hammer

Fits in a
6 ½" × 4 ¾"
(17 × 12 cm)
envelope

Procrastinator's Birthday Greeting

It's never too late to send this well-intentioned, but tardy, turtle card.

1. In your word processing or page layout program, create a rectangle 3 ½" × 2 ½" (9 × 6 cm).

2. In all-caps 12-point Papyrus font, write the words "HAPPY BELATED BIRTHDAY" on the lower one-third of the rectangle. Color the type dark green.

3. Trim the light green paint-textured paper down to 8 ½" × 11" (22 × 28 cm) and place it in your printer. Print out the "HAPPY BELATED BIRTHDAY" document and trim it down to size using the rotary trimmer or scalloped-edged scissors.

4. Using the copper inkpad, stamp a turtle about ¼" (6 mm) above the type centering it on the page.

5. Cut out a tiny triangle from the gold portion of the Joss paper to make a party hat for the turtle. Glue it onto the top of the turtle's head.

6. Glue the Joss paper onto the remaining paint texture paper or any medium-weight paper. This will make the Joss paper sturdier. Trim the reinforced Joss paper down to 5⅛" × 4" (13 × 10 cm).

7. Glue the turtle and birthday greeting card onto the Joss paper, centering it in the gold portion of the Joss paper.

8. Cut out a 6" × 9" (15 × 23 cm) piece of the green corrugated cardboard and fold it in half so it measures 6" × 4 ½" (15 × 11 cm).

9. Center then glue the Joss paper/turtle card to the green corrugated card.

10. Using the screw punch, make four holes, one in each corner of the Joss paper, going through all the layers in the front of the card.

11. Place the eyelets in the holes, decorative sides on the front of the card.

12. Flip the card to the inside front cover and use the eyelet-setting tool and a hammer to splay and set the edges of the eyelets.

VARIATION >> *Use a rabbit rubber stamp instead of a turtle and typeset the words "GET WELL SOON" on the front of the card.*

materials

~ white printer paper
~ newspaper
~ 8 ½" × 11"
  (22 × 28 cm)
  Lokta Natura paper
~ word processing
  software
  (MS Word)
~ computer
~ printer
~ metal ruler
~ pencil
~ paintbrush
~ white glue
~ photocopier

Fits in a #10 envelope

Eliza's News Stationery

Extra, Extra! Read all about the news that fits onto a letter-sized sheet.

1. Using your favorite word processing software and printer, typeset your title on the upper 2" (5 cm) of your 8 ½" × 11" (22 × 28 cm) document. ("Eliza's News" is 50-point Times New Roman centered.) Once set, print out onto white printer paper.

2. Lightly sketch a line 2" (5 cm) from top of paper.

3. Tear pieces of newspaper into small bits. Using your paintbrush, coat the backs of your newspaper pieces with glue, and adhere them to the top of the printer paper, staying within the line you sketched. Completely cover the area, overlapping pieces of newspaper.

4. Carefully tear around the type, getting as close to the type as you can.

5. Set the copy machine to text mode and print as many copies as you need onto the Lokta Natura paper.

ARTIST: ANDY MCFADDEN (THIS PAGE); JEANINE STEIN (OPPOSITE PAGE)

Cocktail Party Invitation with Tunes to Go

This recycled CD cover gets your guests excited about your next bash with some music they can listen to in advance.

1. Select areas on old record album covers that you'd like to use for the invitations, one for the front, one for the back.

2. Using a craft knife and metal ruler, cut the sections of the album covers down to 5 ½" (14 cm) square.

3. Bind the covers together using a strip of self-adhesive bookcloth cut 1" × 11½" (3 × 29 cm), in a color that coordinates with the record album. Regular bookcloth can also be used, but it must be glued. Leave a ¼" (6 mm) gap between the covers. When wrapping the book cloth around the covers, make sure the ends meet on the inside of the invitation.

4. Cut the Mi-tientes inner paper using the CD template. Make all scores and folds. For the pocket, fold up the tabs and glue them in place. Attach this to the inside of the covers with the pocket on the left-hand side.

5. Print the invitation and the note about the CD on coordinating card stock. Attach to the inside using photo corners.

6. Using the CD as a cutting guide, cut coordinating paper to cover. A circle cutter can also be used for this. Attach to the underside of the CD using spray adhesive.

7. Print "You're Invited" on coordinating paper and attach it to a clear epoxy pebble. Attach the pebble to the cover of the invitation.

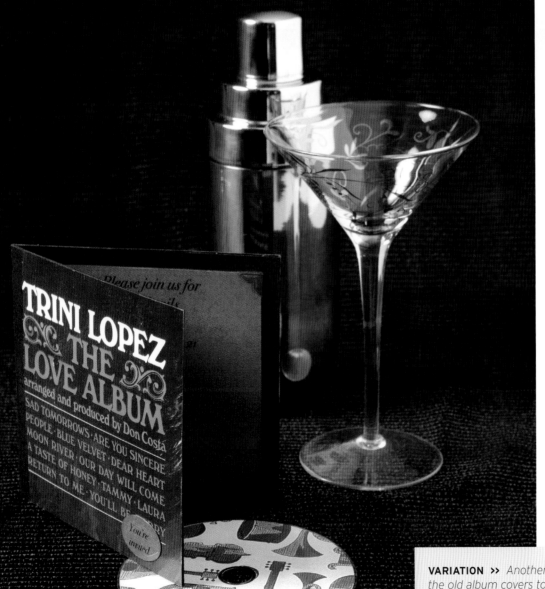

materials

- ~ downloadable template: Cocktail Party CD *(See page 18 for instructions.)*
- ~ old record albums
- ~ self-adhesive bookcloth
- ~ Canson Mi-tientes paper
- ~ card stock (for the invitation and CD note)
- ~ clear epoxy pebbles
- ~ metal ruler
- ~ craft knife
- ~ cutting mat
- ~ glue stick or double-sided tape
- ~ photo corners
- ~ spray adhesive

For extra protection, send the invitation out in a small padded envelope.

VARIATION >> *Another easy way to do this is to glue the old album covers to an existing plastic CD holder.*

Monogrammed and Stitched Portfolio

Quiet pastels meet hard geometric shapes to make this soft, modern writing assortment.

ARTIST: JEANINE STEIN

For the portfolio:

1. Trace the edges of the Monogrammed Stationery Portfolio template on the back side of the large sheet of cream-colored card stock. Cut to fit. Score and fold in the edges until the front flaps of the portfolio meet.

2. For the front panels, cut two pieces of the decorative card stock 4" × 11" (10 × 28 cm) and stitch around the perimeter, using the method described for the stationery. Stitch in two pieces of 12" (30 cm) ribbon on the back of the decorative card stock. Make sure these pieces are facing each other; they will be used to tie the portfolio. Adhere the panels to the front doors of the portfolio. Trim the monogram to about 2¾" × 1¾" (7 × 5 cm). Mat that onto another piece of paper. Center the piece and adhere it to the left panel of the portfolio only.

3. Make an additional two panels for the inside of the portfolio, following the directions above, but leave off the ribbon. Attach these to the inside flaps.

For the portfolio pocket:

1. Place the Monogrammed Stationery Portfolio Pocket template over a sheet of decorative card stock. Cut to fit. Stitch around the front of the pocket using the method described for the stationery. Score, then accordion fold in the left and right sides of the pocket. Score then fold up the bottom flap. Adhere the pocket to the inside of the portfolio. Place the stationery and envelopes inside.

For the envelopes and envelope seals:

1. Trace Monogrammed Stationery Envelope template onto the back of the decorative card stock and cut out. Make score marks with a scoring tool, and fold. Using the method described above for stitching, stitch around the front of the envelope. Adhere flaps with glue stick. For envelope seals, trim monograms to about 2½" × 1½" (6 × 4 cm), and stitch around the border, using the method described for the stationery. Do not do zigzag stitches on the seals.

For the stationery:

1. Trim the decorative card stock to 7" × 10" (18 × 25 cm).

2. Create an 8½" × 11" (22 × 28 cm) document in your page layout or word processing program. Set the monograms on the computer using various fonts and print them onto the decorative paper. Trim the monograms down to 2" × 1" (5 × 3 cm).

3. Place a touch of glue stick onto the back of the monogram top and adhere it to the top center of the 7" × 10" (18 × 25 cm) card. This helps to hold it in place as you stitch.

4. Set the sewing machine to a running stitch and, starting in one corner, stitch a wavy border around the paper.

5. Make a second pass around the border, and crisscross your stitches to create small, open areas.

6. Set the machine to a zigzag setting and stitch in random areas around the paper. Tie off all the loose threads on the back of the paper.

materials

- ~ downloadable templates: Monogrammed Stationery Envelope, Monogrammed Stationery Portfolio, Monogrammed Stationery Portfolio Pocket *(See page 18 for instructions.)*
- ~ various 8½" × 11" (22 × 28 cm) coordinating decorative card stocks *(Luxe-Diamonds, Dots, Stripes, and Glass Dots)*
- ~ 8½" × 11" (22 × 28 cm) card stock in various pastel shades
- ~ large sheet of cream-colored card stock *(portfolio)*

- ~ metal ruler
- ~ craft knife
- ~ cutting mat
- ~ sewing machine
- ~ coordinating thread
- ~ coordinating ribbon
- ~ scoring tool
- ~ glue stick
- ~ computer
- ~ word processing or page layout program *(MS Word or Quark XPress)*

Instructions include custom-made envelopes to match.

**TIP ›› ** *Use contrasting thread to make the stitches stand out. Use a neutral-colored bobbin thread for all sewing.*

materials

- ~ 8 ½" × 11" (22 × 28 cm) card stock in coordinating color *(turquoise)*
- ~ 1 sheet of coordinating felt *(turquoise)*
- ~ flower pin
- ~ 2 buttons in coordinating colors
- ~ metal ruler
- ~ craft knife
- ~ cutting mat
- ~ sewing machine
- ~ coordinating thread *(dark blue)*
- ~ fabric glue
- ~ computer
- ~ word processing or page layout software *(MS Word or Quark XPress)*
- ~ printer
- ~ white inkjet paper
- ~ adhesive hook and loop dots *(Velcro)*
- ~ scissors
- ~ zigzag or scallop-edged scissors

Fits in a 6 ½" × 4 ¾" (17 × 12 cm) envelope

Extra, Extra, Happy Mother's Day Pin Card

Flower pins are all the rage these days. Why not create a card that packages both the card and present together?

1. Cut out a rectangle from the card stock: 9" × 6½" (23 × 17 cm) then score and fold the card in half to measure 4 ½" × 6" (11 × 15 cm).

2. Cut out a rectangle of felt 9" × 6 ½" (23 × 17 cm) and fold that in half the same way and mark the halfway point.

3. Sew all of the right edge and one-half of the top edge of the felt with a zig-zag stitch, placing the needle about ⅜" (2 cm) from the edge.

4. Glue the unstitched half of the card to the front of the folded card stock and fold the upper right-hand corner on the diagonal to form a lapel (see photo).

5. Glue the lapel edge into place.

6. Sew two buttons on the right front side of the felted part of the card as shown in photo.

7. Adhere two Velcro dots—one on the back side of the front flap directly on top of the knotted thread from the buttons and the other on the card itself. This will adhere the front part of the jacket to the back part of the jacket.

8. Create a new document in your word processing or page layout program, 2" × ¾" (5 × 2 cm) and set the following phrases (all centered, 11-point Gill Sans upper- and lowercase letters): for line 1 "XX Happy Mother's Day"; line 2: "100% Super Human"; line 3: "Hand wash only." Do not press.; line 4: No bleach except on hair. Note: Lines 2-4 should be set in 7-point Gill Sans upper- and lowercase letters.

9. Print the tag and trim the bottom edge with zigzag or scallop-edged scissors. Sew seams on the left and right sides of the paper tag, then glue the tag onto the card.

Simple Sewn Stationery

Make a plain envelope and sheet of letterhead come to life with a sewn edge and some elegant paper.

1. In a blank Word document, choose File ➡ Page Setup ➡ Margins tab. Set margins as follows: top 0.25, bottom 0.25, left 0, and right 1.5.

2. On the information bar at the bottom of the screen, hit "enter" until you reach line position 0.2. Type in your address in two centered lines.

3. At line position 10.2, type in your name, centered. Sample uses Carpenter ITG 24-point for the name and 18-point for the address. Select File ➡ Print. If you get a margin alert that asks if you want to continue with print, click "yes." The document should print with the address line very close to the top and the name about ½" (1 cm) up from the bottom.

4. Trim 1 ½" (4 cm) off the right-hand side of the sheet so it now measures 7" x 11" (18 x 28 cm). From the top, measure down 4" (10 cm), then score and fold. From the bottom, measure up 2" (5 cm), then score and fold so that the name is on the top flap and covers the address when folded closed.

5. With the top flap of the sheet folded down, stitch one torn piece of decorative paper across the top through both layers of paper. Keep the stitching ¼" (6 mm) from the fold and the decorative paper clearing the printed name. Repeat the same process on the back flap of the envelope, stitching on the flap only. Place the 7" x 7" (18 x 18 cm) decorative paper inside the envelope as a lining and trim the paper on the flap to fit envelope configuration. Adhere liner to flap with double-sided tape.

ARTIST: MARY LAWLER

materials

~ 8½" x 11" (22 x 28 cm) pearl paper 120 g (Canson Effects)

~ 5" x 7" (13 x 18 cm) pearl envelope (Canson Effects)

~ 8½" x 11" (22 x 28 cm) decorative paper cut down to 7" (18 cm) square

~ 8½" x 11" (22 x 28 cm) decorative paper ripped down into two pieces ¾" x 8" (2 x 20 cm)

~ matching thread

~ sewing machine with decorative stitch selection

~ word processing program (MS Word)

Fits in a #10 envelope

TIP ➤➤ *Experiment on a blank sheet of paper to get the stitch style that works best with your papers.*

materials

- ~ brown card stock
- ~ orange striped decorative paper
- ~ 1" × 2" (3 × 5 cm) silver scrapbooking frame
- ~ catalog pages
- ~ yellow dots paper
- ~ bottle cap
- ~ orange button
- ~ scrapbook fastener
- ~ metal ruler
- ~ craft knife
- ~ cutting mat
- ~ bone folder
- ~ deckled-edged scissors
- ~ craft glue
- ~ glue stick
- ~ word processing software (MS Word)
- ~ computer
- ~ printer
- ~ drinking glass
- ~ hammer
- ~ nail

Fits in a 6" × 9"
(15 × 23 cm) envelope

Recycled Thank-You Card

A bottle cap, a button, and a catalog mix it up with some newer materials to create this mixed-media card.

1. Cut out a sheet of brown card stock 11" × 8 ½" (28 × 22 cm). Score then fold the card in half so it measures 5 ¾" × 8 ½" (15 × 22 cm). Use a bone folder to make the edges crisp.

2. Cut out an orange striped sheet of paper 5" × 8" (13 × 20 cm) and deckle the edges with the scissors.

3. Adhere the orange sheet to the front of the folded brown card.

4. Using word processing software and printer, typeset then print out the words "THANK YOU" in all caps in white on a black background to fit onto a 1½" × 1" (3.5 × 3 cm) rectangle. Cut out the rectangle and adhere it to the orange striped sheet about 1" (3 cm) in from the right side and bottom of the card.

5. Adhere a metal frame on top of your message.

6. Cut out a 6½" (17 cm) stem with leaves from the yellow dots paper. Make snips along the edges of the leaves with your scissors to give the leaves dimension.

7. Glue the stem onto the page leaving space on top for the flower.

8. Place a 2½" 6 cm) diameter glass over an interesting image in your catalog. Here, we've placed it over an image of flowered sheets to match the theme. Using a craft knife, cut around the glass and through about five layers of the catalog. Set aside.

9. Hammer a hole into the middle of the bottle cap with the nail.

10. Place the fastener through the bottle cap and the center of the catalog circles and splay the edges of the fastener.

11. Make tiny snips around the edges of the circles with your scissors. Bend the edges of the flower upward with your fingers to give it dimension.

12. Glue the flower on top of the stem and then glue a button into the center of the flower.

VARIATION » *Use corrugated cardboard in the background instead of the orange striped paper.*

4 >> Digital Designs

Computer-Generated Designs

Mod Quad Stationery

Simple geometry plays an important role in this hip-to-be-square letterhead treatment.

1. Create a 6¾" × 9¼" (17 × 23.5 cm) page in your page layout program.

2. Download and import the template.

3. Print the document onto 8½" × 11" (22 × 28 cm) bright white paper and trim it to the crop marks.

4. Punch the corners with the rounded corner punch.

materials

~ downloadable templates: Mod Quad, Mod Quad Variation *(See page 18 for instructions.)*

~ 8½" x 11" (22 x 28 cm) super-fine white paper

~ computer

~ page layout program *(Quark XPress)*

~ metal ruler

~ craft knife

~ cutting mat

~ rounded corner punch *(Marvy)*

Fits in an A7 envelope

VARIATION » *Use the alternate full page Mod Quad template to print an entire sheet. Follow the same instructions but fold the card (also shown in photo) in half vertically before rounding out the corners with the punch.*

materials

~ downloadable templates: Boomerang, Boomerang Variation *(See page 18 for instructions.)*

~ 8½" x 11" (22 x 28 cm) buff white paper

~ computer

~ page layout program *(Quark XPress)*

~ printer

~ metal ruler

~ craft knife

~ cutting mat

~ rounded corner craft punch

Fits in an A7 envelope

Boomerang Letterhead and Notecards

This updated design reminiscent of your grandmother's countertop is a blast from the past.

1. Create a 6¾" x 9¼" (17 x 23.5 cm) document in your page layout program.

2. Download the boomerang template or create your own boomerang shapes with the vector tool in your page layout program.

3. Place the template at the top of the page, leaving a little part of the template outside of the page edge for trimming.

4. Print the page on the buff white paper and trim it to the crop marks.

5. Punch out the corners with the rounded corner punch.

VARIATION >> *Use the alternate full page Boomerang template to print an entire sheet. Follow the same instructions but fold the card (also shown in photo) in half vertically before rounding out the corners with the punch.*

materials

~ downloadable
  template: Hollow Man
  *(See page 18 for
  instructions.)*

~ 8½" × 11"
  (22 × 28 cm)
  white card stock

~ computer

~ scanning software
  (Photoshop)

~ color printer

~ metal ruler

~ craft knife

~ cutting mat

Fits in a 5" × 7"
(13 × 18 cm) envelope

MISSING YOU

Hollow Man Card

This simple use of negative space conveys how you feel
about that special someone not being in the picture.

1. Open the Hollow Man template in your scanning program.

2. Print the template out onto the white card stock and trim
   to the crop marks. Cut the man shape out of the front
   cover with the craft knife.

3. Fold the card in half.

VARIATION >> *Draw a dotted line around the outside of the man to push this concept one step further.*

Cut Out for Motherhood

This modern take on a baby's arrival is a great way to congratulate couples on their up-and-coming parenthood.

1. Open the Motherhood template in your scanning program.

2. Print the template out onto the white card stock and trim to the crops. Cut the woman shape out of the front cover with the craft knife. Punch out the hole above her head.

3. Fold the card in half.

4. Draw then cut out a ⅞" (2 cm) circle around the baby photo. Glue the baby face photo onto the tag. If you have more than one copy, glue one photo to the front of the tag and one to the back.

5. Double thread a needle with the neutral-colored thread and puncture a hole into the top of the tag. Tie a knot about ¼" (6 mm) above the tag and thread the needle through the hole in the top of the card. Tie the thread in a knot and trim the ends.

materials

~ downloadable template: Motherhood *(See page 18 for instructions.)*

~ 8 ½" × 11" (22 × 28 cm) white card stock

~ 1" (3 cm) metal tag

~ 1 or 2 baby face photos to fit a 1" (3 cm) metal tag

~ computer

~ scanning software (Photoshop)

~ color printer

~ hole or drill punch

~ metal ruler

~ craft knife

~ cutting mat

~ circle guide

~ glue stick

~ neutral-colored thread

~ sewing needle

Fits in a 5" × 7" (13 × 18 cm) envelope

Ben's Bowl-o-Rama Birthday Invitation

Who can resist putting their fingers through this bowling ball? This interactive card will get your guests excited about your birthday blowout.

1. Set up an 8½" × 11" (22 × 28 cm) document in your word processing program.

2. Center the type for the invitation in the middle of the page. To create the arc effect in the headline, we used the curving graphic feature from the Word Art Gallery (MS Word program). We chose the T Impact font, 24-point. We added the red outline by using the outline feature from the Format ➡ Font menu. For the body type, we used 9-point Arial and we colorized the text in blues, greens, and reds.

3. Add a placeholder circle in your document for the text to print on the circle sticker, which will happen in the following steps.

4. Print the document onto the printer paper and then tape one of the cream circle stickers over the placeholder on the printed sheet.

5. Run the sheet through the printer a second time. This time the graphic should print directly onto the sticker.

6. Take the sticker off the 8½" × 11" (22 × 28 cm) sheet and adhere it to the black circle card.

7. Punch three holes through the cards to make it look like a bowling ball.

8. Place the invitation in the envelope and seal it with a 1" (3 cm) black sticker on the back flap.

materials

~ 8½" × 11" (22 × 28 cm) white printer paper

~ 5½" (14 cm) black circle cards

~ 5" (13 cm) cream circle stickers

~ 1" (3 cm) black circle stickers

~ computer

~ word processing program (MS Word)

~ printer

~ ½" (1 cm) hole punch

~ tape

Fits in a 5 ¾" (15 cm) square envelope

VARIATION >> *Place some funky bowling stickers on the front or back of the envelope.*

~ black 4-bar rounded photo frame cards

~ 1" (3 cm) square lenticular printed "Yes" or "No" image

~ 5" × 3½" (13 × 9 cm) red sheet of paper

~ craft glue

~ glue stick

~ computer

~ page layout or word processing software (*Quark XPress* or *MS Word*)

~ printer

~ white adhesive-back printer paper

~ craft knife

~ cutting mat

Fits in a 4-bar envelope

Should I Stay or Should I Go Now? Invitation

A lenticular printed "Yes" and "No" is a fun teaser for your next party

1. Open out a photo frame card onto your work surface.

2. Glue the red sheet of paper to the inside center panel with the glue stick.

3. Adhere the "Yes" and "No" image into the inside panel of the card, centering it in the photo frame.

4. Set the typography ½" (1 cm) in from the left-hand side of a 3½" × 5" (9 × 13 cm) page for the outside of the invitation as follows:

   For the "YES" and "NO (check one)": 15-point Akzidenz Grotesque Light on a leading of 16 points.

5. For the rest of the copy: 10 point Akzidenz Grotesque Light on a leading of 11. White Bullets are Zapf Dingbats (keystroke 'n'.)

6. Color the background black and the type white.

7. Output onto the white adhesive-backed paper.

8. Trim to fit front cover of the photo frame card. Adhere the invitation to the front of the card. Cut out opening around the exterior window of the card.

VARIATION >> *A variety of lenticular images exists in the marketplace. Use your imagination to make an originalinvitation or card that suits your theme.*

ARTIST: DEBORAH BASKIN

materials

~ downloadable template: Vintage Candy Tin *(See page 18 for instructions.)*

~ vintage candy tin

~ 8 ½" × 11" (22 × 28 cm) cream-colored card stock

~ 8 ½" × 11" (22 × 28 cm) adhesive-backed paper

~ computer

~ scanner

~ scanning software *(Photoshop)*

~ color printer

~ metal ruler

~ craft knife

~ cutting mat

~ glue stick

~ pencil

~ rotary paper trimmer with deckled-edge blade

Fits in a 5 ¾" × 4 ⅜" (15 × 11 cm) envelope

Vintage Candy Tin with Stationery

By scanning the lid of a lovely old tin, you've got the artwork for your stationery and a place in which to store it.

1. Create a new document in your scanning software package measuring 5½" × 8½" (14 × 22 cm).

2. Scan the lid of the candy tin at 100 percent and place in your document, using the scale tool to make it fit a width of about 5" (13 cm).

3. Place the image on the lower half of the page.

4. Open the Print dialog box and check the boxes for registration marks, corner crop marks, and center crop marks before you send the job to print.

5. Print the stationery on the cream-colored card stock.

6. Score the center of the card. Fold the card in half and then trim out the cards with the rotary paper trimmer.

7. Line the tin with colored raffia or make a box insert to hold the cards.

VARIATION ›› *For both projects, you can use the online templates and forgo the matching tins.*

Lady Liberty Tin with Stationery

Just as this statue was originally presented to the United States from France, you can use this smaller-scale version as a gift to your loved ones.

1. Create a new 12" × 6" (30 × 15 cm) document in your scanning software package.

2. Scan the lid of the candy tin at 100 percent and place it in your document, using the scale tool to make it fit on one-half (6" [15 cm]) the width of the page. Place the image on the right half of the page.

3. Print the stationery on the watercolor paper, making sure to change the printer format to 8½" × 14" (22 × 36 cm) paper in your print dialogue box.

4. Score the center of the card. Fold the card in half on the score line, then cut the card out, trimming the card around the octagonal box shape except in the center fold area.

5. Using the screw punch, create a hole about ¾" (2 cm) in from the right-hand side of the card, centering it on the top and bottom and making sure to pierce through both layers of the card with the screw punch.

6. With the circle punch, cut out two red cardboard circles. Make a hole in the center of each of these circles with the screw punch.

7. Align the red cardboard circle on top the hole on the front of the card and place the screw through both, decorative side of the screw facing out.

8. Open the card and set the screw in place with the eyelet-setting tool and hammer. Repeat this same process on the back of the card.

9. Wrap the card with a piece of embroidery thread, starting from the back to front of the card. Twist the thread underneath both of the red cardboard circles.

10. Line the tin with raffia.

materials

~ downloadable template: Lady Liberty (See page 18 for instructions.)

~ vintage candy tin

~ 8½" × 14" (22 × 36 cm) sheet of cream-colored watercolor paper

~ a scrap of deep red card stock

~ red raffia

~ ¼" (6 mm) brass-colored screws

~ red embroidery thread

~ screw punch

~ eyelet-setting tool

~ hammer

~ craft knife

~ metal ruler

~ ½" (1 cm) circle punch

~ computer

~ scanner

~ scanning software (Photoshop)

~ color printer

Fits in a 6½" (17 cm) square envelope

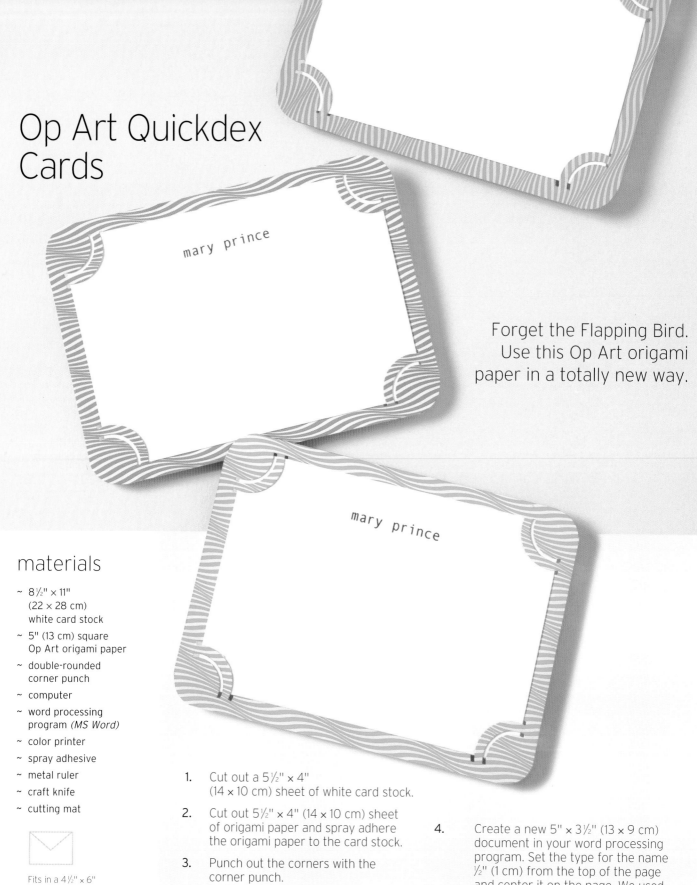

Op Art Quickdex Cards

Forget the Flapping Bird. Use this Op Art origami paper in a totally new way.

materials

~ 8½" × 11" (22 × 28 cm) white card stock

~ 5" (13 cm) square Op Art origami paper

~ double-rounded corner punch

~ computer

~ word processing program (MS Word)

~ color printer

~ spray adhesive

~ metal ruler

~ craft knife

~ cutting mat

Fits in a 4½" × 6" (11 × 15 cm) envelope

VARIATION >> Change the dimensions of the origami card and use it to house photographs or tickets.

1. Cut out a 5½" × 4" (14 × 10 cm) sheet of white card stock.

2. Cut out 5½" × 4" (14 × 10 cm) sheet of origami paper and spray adhere the origami paper to the card stock.

3. Punch out the corners with the corner punch.

4. Create a new 5" × 3½" (13 × 9 cm) document in your word processing program. Set the type for the name ½" (1 cm) from the top of the page and center it on the page. We used 15-point Ayuthaya for our text.

5. Print the card out on the white card stock and trim it out. Place the white card in the corners of the origami card.

Gnome Man Is an Island

Which is exactly why you should send this message out to your friend or family member. Cake decorations and a scanner are just about all you need to make this friendly little elf come to life.

1. Place the gnome on the scanner with a white piece of paper behind him. Scan at 200%. You may have to clean up the edges with the eraser tool to make the image neat and clean.

2. Create a new 3¾" × 9¼" (10 × 23.5 cm) document in your scanning software package. Place the gnome on the page and scale him up until he's about 3 ¼" (8.5 cm) tall.

3. Create a cartoon bubble with the oval tool in the upper left-hand corner. Pull down the edit menu and go to the Stroke menu. Give the oval a line weight of 3 pixels. Fill it with white. Start a new layer. Use the polygonal lasso tool to make a triangle pointing to the gnome's mouth and give that a line weight of 3 pixels and a fill of white. Go back to the bubble layer. Using the polygonal lasso tool, highlight the area where the oval and the triangle overlap, then hit the delete key. This should make it a complete thought bubble.

4. Print the card onto the #10 flat card.

materials

~ gnome cake decoration
~ superfine white #10 flat cards
~ adhesive-backed paper
~ computer
~ scanning software (Photoshop)
~ color scanner

Fits in a #10 envelope

OPTIONAL STEP » *For added fun, make a whole 8½" × 11" (22 × 28 cm) sheet of gnome stickers by placing the gnome on a new page in your scanning software package and scaling him down to 1½" (4 cm) high. Duplicate him many times on the page and print the page out onto an 8½" × 11" (22 × 28 cm) sheet of adhesive-backed paper. Cut around the shape of the gnome and place him on the envelope flap. You can also make a cigar band with decorative paper and the gnome stickers placed randomly to the band.*

Oodles of Poodles Stationery

Parlez vous poodle? To open this letter, the recipient has to unhook the chain from the dog's collar.

1. Load the printer with a sheet of the slab scrapbook paper that has been cut down to 8 ½" × 11" (22 × 28 cm).

2. Open and print the template. You may have to set the printer up to print on legal size to avoid the image getting chopped off on the sides.

3. Trim the card and fold in the front flaps of the card, which contain the dog and dog walker on the fronts.

4. Cut a 3" (8 cm) length of chain, and add an eye pin to the last link of the chain. You will have to open and then close the circle portion of the eye pin with the needle-nose pliers in order to get it on the chain. Cut the end of the eye pin so it measures about ¾" (2 cm) long. Bend the stick portion of the eye pin into a hook shape.

5. Place a minibrad through the chain, then pierce the brad through the card under the dog walker's hand (see photo) and splay and flatten the brad points on the inside of the card.

6. Make a chain of two jump rings, squeezing them together with the needle-nose pliers. Place a brad through the middle of one of the jump rings and pierce the brad through the right-hand side of the dog's collar (see photo). Splay and flatten the brad points.

7. Hook the leash onto the dog's collar by placing the hook through the jump ring.

Fits in a 5 ½" × 4 ¼" (14 × 10.5 cm) envelope

materials

- downloadable template: Oodles of Poodles *(See page 18 for instructions.)*
- 12" (30 cm) square slab scrapbook papers in stripes, dots, and swirls
- silver necklace chain
- 2 silver-colored minibrads for scrapbook making
- jewelry-making eye pins
- 2 jump rings
- computer
- page layout program *(Quark XPress)*
- printer
- metal ruler
- craft knife
- cutting mat
- needle-nose pliers

VARIATION >> *Use a 12 mm lobster clasp for a more secure closure.*

Fashion Statement Envelope and Stationery

Use funky wrapping paper to make envelopes that will set your letter apart from the myriad plain, white rectangles that stream through the mail slot.

For the stationery:

1. Create a 5" × 7" (13 × 18 cm) word processing document. Import the stock art of the lady into your document and scale it to 1½" (4 cm) tall, leaving ½" (1 cm) on the top and left sides of the document.

2. Write the words, "I am woman! I am invincible! I am pooped!" in 7-point serif italic type under the stock art of the lady. Add "–writer unknown" in 5-point all-caps serif type under the quote.

3. Print out your document onto the pink card stock and trim.

4. Using pink thread, make a zigzag stitch on the right and bottom sides of your card, leaving ⅝" (1.5 cm) on both edges.

For the envelope:

1. Carefully open the seams of an A7 envelope and then tape to the back of a sheet of wrapping paper. Trace the outline of the envelope onto the back of the sheet of the wrapping paper with a pencil. This will be your template.

2. Remove the A7 envelope and cut the envelope template out of the wrapping paper using the craft knife.

3. Fold and glue the inside edges of the bottom outside panels, placing and adhering the bottom middle panel of the envelope on top of the other two panels.

4. Fold in the top panel of the envelope.

5. After you've completed your letter and are ready to seal, you can glue the top panel with the glue stick.

materials

- downloadable template: Fashion Statement (*See page 18 for instructions.*)
- 1 sheet of Vintage Fashion Catalog wrapping paper
- 8½" × 11" (22 × 28 cm) deep pink card stock
- 1 A7 envelope (*any color*)
- craft knife
- metal ruler
- glue stick
- sewing machine
- pink sewing thread
- word processing program (*MS Word*)
- pencil

You can make the customized A7 envelope described in the directions above.

VARIATION >> *Try a variety of different stitches and various colors of thread on your sewing machine to achieve some different looks.*

materials

~ downloadable template: Hello Notecard *(See page 18 for instructions.)*

~ 8½" × 11" (22 × 28 cm) sheet of dark red ribbed cardboard

~ 8½" × 11" (22 × 28 cm) cream-colored paper

~ computer

~ page layout program *(Quark XPress)*

~ color printer

~ metal ruler

~ craft knife

~ cutting mat

~ 1 bull-nose clip

Hello Notecards

When you need to send off a quick note, these industrial strength notecards will do the trick.

1. Cut a 6¾" × 4¾" (17 × 12 cm) rectangle out of the ribbed cardboard.

2. Create a 6¼" × 4¼" (16 × 11 cm) page in your page layout program.

3. Download and then import the Hello Notecard template and scale it down to 1" (3 cm).

4. Center the hello graphic and position it about ½" (1 cm) from the top of the page.

5. Create the dotted lines for the message about 1¾" (5 cm) down from the top of the page, ⅜" (2 cm) apart from one another and about ½" (1 cm) from the sides of the page.

6. Referring to the photograph for placement, use American Typewriter font and add "from me:" and "when:" on the first line; "to you:" on the second line.

7. Print at least ten copies on the cream stock and trim them out.

8. Clip the notes and the ribbed cardboard together with the bull-nose clip.

VARIATION >> *Use this same idea as a message pad to place next to your telephone by slightly changing the words as desired.*

Happy New Year from Luka

Dots filled with color, typography, and baby bring in
the new year with style.

1. Create a new 6 ¾" × 4 ¾"
   (17 × 12 cm) document in your page
   layout program.

2. Create a grid of seven dots across the
   page and five dots down for a total of
   thirty-five dots.

3. Color the background dark red.
   Colorize the dots bright red and olive
   green.

4. Import six of your favorite baby
   photos into the dots, placing them in
   a random fashion around the page.

5. Add the typography in white into
   the dots.

6. Use the vector drawing tool to create
   starbursts around the page and scale
   them up and down in size in a hap-
   hazard fashion until you get the look
   you want.

ARTIST: ALLYSON ROSS

materials

~ downloadable template:
  Happy New Year
  *(see page 18 for
  instructions)*

~ 8 ½" × 11" (22 × 28 cm)
  matte photo paper

~ craft knife

~ cutting mat

~ computer

~ scanning program
  (Photoshop)

~ page layout program

Fits in a 4 ½" × 6 ½"
(11 × 17 cm) envelope

EASY ALTERNATIVE » *Open the Happy New Year template and place your type and photos on top of that.*

People Post-Its

This quadrant of brightly colored, sticky notepads is a great way to display your best photos and jot down a phone number. When one of the mini-notepads runs out, replace it with a new one.

materials

~ four 3" × 3" (8 × 8 cm) sticky notepads in green, yellow, orange, and purple

~ piece of cardboard cut down to 6" (15 cm) square

~ 4 black-and-white photographs

~ 8½" × 11" (22 × 28 cm) inkjet vellum

~ computer

~ scanner

~ scanning software (Photoshop)

~ printer

~ cutting mat

~ metal ruler

~ craft knife

~ glue stick

~ double-sided tape

~ bone folder

1. Place some double-sided tape to the back of each of the four sticky notepads and adhere them to the cardboard, two on top, two on the bottom.

2. Scan the four black-and-white photos into your computer.

3. Create a 6" (15 cm) square in your scanning software package and place the photos within the space so there are two on top and two on the bottom, making a quadrant. Each photo should measure 3" (8 cm) square. Scale the faces up or down within the 3" space, so that it makes an interesting composition and not all of the faces are the exact same size.

4. Add a black horizontal line and a vertical line and a black button in the middle with the person's (or people's) name(s) written in the middle in white type. We used 12- on 12-point American Typewriter bold.

5. Print the sheet at 101 percent onto the inkjet vellum.

6. Cut the sheet down to fit, leaving about 3" (8 cm) on the top to wrap around the top of the notepad.

7. Fold the top edges of the vellum with the bone folder so it wraps crisply around the notepads.

8. Glue the vellum to the back side of the notepad.

TIP ›› *This is an inexpensive and fabulous gift for any occasion such as birthdays, holidays, or even as a wedding favor.*

Carolynn's Excellent Adventure Cards

An i-Zone camera and some photo corners make these vacation cards a snap to produce.

1. Scan the i-Zone or comparable photo on the scanner and size it up to roughly 3 ¼" × 5" (8.5 × 13 cm). Crop the photos leaving at least a ⅛" (3 mm) border of black around the edges of the photo.

2. Print the photos on the photo paper and trim them out leaving at least an ⅛" (3 mm) border of black around the edges of the photo.

3. Place the photo in the center of the card and adhere it to the card with the photo corners.

ARTIST: CAROLYNN DECILLO

materials

~ i-Zone camera and film
~ black photo corners
~ pool blue foldover cards
~ 8 ½" × 11" (22 × 28 cm) matte photo paper
~ computer
~ scanning software
~ scanner
~ color inkjet or laser printer
~ metal ruler
~ craft knife
~ cutting mat

Fits in a 6 ¾" × 4 ¾" (17 × 12 cm) envelope

VARIATION » *Mount a small metal frame on the front of the card and place the original i-Zone photo in the slot.*

Pink Elephants on Parade Invitation

This updated version of a playful elephant and champagne glass is elevated to a new level with a 3D beaded collar and a sequin eye.

1. Create a new 4½" × 6" (11 × 15 cm) document in your page layout program.

2. Download and place the elephant template into your page and size it down to 1½" (4 cm) from leg to leg.

3. Set the type for the invitation as follows: 14-point Bernhard Fashion BT for the "It's Party Time!," and 10-point Bernhard Fashion BT on a lead of 24-point for: "Who," "When," "Time," and "RSVP."

4. Print the cards onto the cream stock and trim the edges with the rotary paper trimmer.

5. Cut a small piece of the double-stick adhesive in a curved shaped for the collar, place it on the elephant's neck and press the glass marbles into the adhesive.

6. Glue an acrylic jewel onto the eye of the elephant as shown in the photo.

materials

~ downloadable template: Pink Elephants *(see page 18 for instructions.)*

~ 8 ½" × 11" (22 × 28 cm) cream-colored card stock

~ tiny pink glass marbles

~ clear acrylic jewels

~ computer

~ page layout software *(Quark XPress)*

~ color printer

~ rotary paper trimmer with scalloped-edge blade

~ cutting mat

~ double-stick adhesive sheets

~ craft glue

Fits in a 6 ½" × 4 ¾" (17 × 12 cm) envelope. A vellum envelope is shown here.

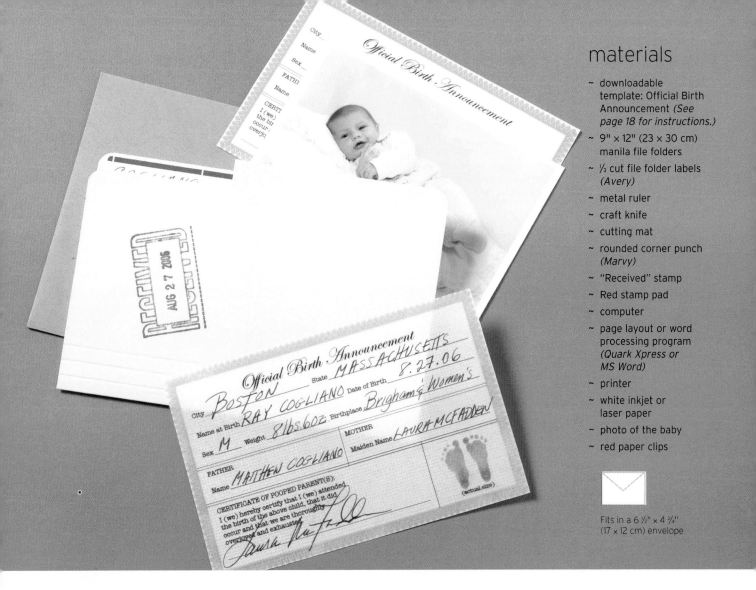

materials

~ downloadable template: Official Birth Announcement *(See page 18 for instructions.)*

~ 9" × 12" (23 × 30 cm) manila file folders

~ ⅓ cut file folder labels *(Avery)*

~ metal ruler

~ craft knife

~ cutting mat

~ rounded corner punch *(Marvy)*

~ "Received" stamp

~ Red stamp pad

~ computer

~ page layout or word processing program *(Quark Xpress or MS Word)*

~ printer

~ white inkjet or laser paper

~ photo of the baby

~ red paper clips

Fits in a 6 ½" × 4 ¾" (17 × 12 cm) envelope

It's Official Birth Announcement

This miniature file is a novel way of letting everyone know about your own little addition.

For the folder:

1. Cut down a full-sized manila folder on the fold line to measure 4 ¼" × 6 ¼" (10.5 × 15.5 cm).

2. Cut a rectangle out of the front of the upper right-hand corner of the folder ¼" × 2" (6 mm × 5 cm) (this will be the area of the folder that exposes your label).

3. Round the top and bottom corners of the folder with the rounded corner punch.

4. Place a label with the baby's last name on it and adhere it to the folder.

5. Use the "received" stamp and inkpad to stamp the outside of the folder.

For the announcement:

1. Create an 11" × 8 ½" (28 × 22 cm) document in your page layout or word processing document. Place the Official Birth Announcement template onto your page and print it onto the white inkjet or laser paper. Then trim it out.

2. Using the paper clips, attach a photo of the baby into the finished folder.

VARIATION >> *For a more hassle-free version, reduce and copy a miniature version of the baby's real birth certificate.*

materials

- ~ downloadable templates: Giant Envelope Stationery Dots, Giant Envelope Stationery Dots Strip *(See page 18 for instructions.)*
- ~ 8 ½" × 11" (22 × 28 cm) laser vellum *(tinted or clear)* or opaque paper
- ~ 9" × 11 ½" (23 × 29 cm) presentation envelope
- ~ computer
- ~ graphic software *(Adobe Photoshop, Illustrator, or other)*
- ~ printer
- ~ craft knife
- ~ cutting mat
- ~ tape

Individual stationery fits in a #10 envelope. The whole set fits in a 9" × 11 ½" (23 × 29 cm) presentation envelope.

Giant Envelope Stationery with Dots

Everything you need to write a letter is inside this big package.

1. Download and open the Giant Envelope Stationery Dots template.

2. Typeset the name, address, and any other pertinent information and place it on the center strip on the page.

3. Print out ten copies of stationery on the vellum.

4. Copy the Giant Envelope Stationery Dots Strip and paste it onto a separate page.

5. Print the page onto the vellum and trim out a narrow strip of paper with the dot pattern on it.

6. Create a band to hold the #10 envelopes by wrapping the narrow strip around the envelopes and securing it to the other end of the strip with a small piece of tape.

7. Place the printed sheets of stationery, bundle of envelopes, and a set of stamps into the giant envelope.

TIP » *You can use any paper or vellum that is compatible with your inkjet or laser printer, but do be sure that it is compatible to prevent smudging.*

ARTIST: ANNA HERRICK (THIS SPREAD)

Giant Envelope Stationery with Stars

An alternative design to the Giant Envelope with Dots.

1. Download and open the Giant Envelope Stationery Stars template.

2. Typeset the name, address, and any other pertinent information and place it under the envelope design on the page.

3. Print out ten copies of stationery onto the vellum.

4. Copy the Giant Stationery Stars Strip and paste it onto a separate page.

5. Print the page onto the vellum and trim out a narrow strip of paper with the dot pattern on it.

6. Create a band to hold the #10 envelopes by wrapping the narrow strip around the envelopes and securing it to the other end of the strip with a small piece of tape.

7. Place the printed sheets of stationery, bundle of envelopes, and a set of stamps into the giant envelope.

ALICE HERRICK
52 VINAL AVE.
SOMERVILLE, MA
02143

materials

~ downloadable templates: Giant Envelope Stationery Stars, Giant Envelope Stationery Stars Strip *(See page 18 for instructions.)*

~ 8½" × 11" (22 × 28 cm) laser vellum *(tinted or clear)* or opaque paper

~ 9" × 11½" (23 × 29 cm) presentation envelope

~ computer

~ graphic software *(Adobe Photoshop, Illustrator, or other)*

~ printer

~ craft knife

~ cutting mat

~ tape

Individual stationery fits in a #10 envelope. The whole set fits in a 9" × 11½" (23 × 29 cm) presentation envelope.

Growing Love Card

An elongated format works well with this thriving hearts plant.

1. Download and open the Growing Love template in your scanning program and print it onto an 11" × 17" (28 × 43 cm) sheet of paper. If you do not have the capability to print it out on that size sheet, spilt up the image, print onto two 8½" × 11" (22 × 28 cm) sheets, and tape together. Or copy it onto a disk and bring it to a copy shop for output.

2. Trim it out to the crops and sign your name.

materials

~ downloadable template: Growing Love *(See page 18 for instructions.)*

~ 11" × 17" (28 × 43 cm) white paper

~ computer

~ scanning program *(Photoshop)*

~ craft knife

~ cutting mat

Fits in a 4 ¾" × 6 ½" (12 × 17 cm) envelope

Who said you can't grow anything?

♥k

HANDMADE OPTION >> *Draw a vine with a fine-tip marker. Add heart stickers and use terra-cotta-colored paper for the pot. Finish it off by hand writing your message.*

03.22.02

03.22.02

04.22.02

06.22.02

We're a few feet behind.
Introducing Avery Rose Miller, born 02.22.02 at 3:33 am
6 pounds 13 ounces, 18.75 inches long

materials

~ downloadable template:
  Baby Feet *(See page 18
  for instructions.)*
~ 11" × 17" (28 × 43 cm)
  white paper
~ computer
~ scanning program
  (Photoshop)
~ craft knife
~ cutting mat
~ bone folder

Fits in a 4 ¾" × 6 ½"
(12 × 17 cm) envelope

A Few
Feet Behind

Quite often, the chaotic
arrival of a new baby leaves
little time to create the
announcement. By showing
the growth of the baby's
foot, you can use the
lapse in time to your
creative advantage.

1. Download and open the Baby Feet template
    in your scanning program.

2. On each panel, set the type for the amount of
    time on that has lapsed since you had the baby.
    On the last panel, set the announcement text.

3. Trim the announcement out using the crops as
    your guide.

4. Lightly score the folds, fold the card into quarters,
    and burnish the folds with the bone folder.

VARIATION » *Scan a photo of the baby and
superimpose it on the big toe on the last panel.*

materials

~ strip of photo booth portraits

~ 8½" × 11" (22 × 28 cm) inkjet or laser compatible photo paper

~ computer

~ scanner

~ scanning software (*Adobe Photoshop*)

~ printer

Fits in a #10 envelope

Photo Booth Stationery

A quick way to make quirky stationery that's both fun and uniquely you

1. Take a strip of three or four pictures taken at an old-fashioned photo booth.

2. Scan the strip of pictures onto your computer.

3. Using a graphics software, place the image of the strip on an 8½" × 11" (22 × 28 cm) page.

4. Typeset your name, address, and any other pertinent information under the photographs. We used 18-point Adriatric .

5. Use the software to decorate and colorize the photos.

6. Print the stationery onto the photo paper.

ALTERNATIVE OPTION >> *Make a card with cut out windows and place the strip of photos behind each of the windows.*

Brown Bag It

This is a crafty invite for those events when guests are asked to bring their own lunch

1. Refer to image of finished card and envelope below.

2. If you wish, typeset information about your event to the right of the bag on the invitation, as shown in the finished card. Or leave that area blank for a handwritten message.

3. Feed an 8½" × 11" (22 × 28 cm) sheet of brown craft paper into your laser or inkjet printer and print the invitation on Template A.

4. Align a craft knife and ruler along the crop marks on Template A and cut out the 6" (15 cm) square invitation out of the brown craft paper.

5. Note the jagged edge on the top of the brown bag on the invitation. Cut along the contour of the jagged edge so that there is zigzag incision along the top of the bag.

6. Feed an 8½" × 11" (22 × 28 cm) sheet of white paper into your laser or inkjet printer and print the food, grass, and label artwork on Template B. If you wish, typeset the name of the recipient on the label before printing.

7. Cut out the artwork of the bread, apple, cheese, and wine bottle. Tip: You can cut out the artwork provided on Template B and paste it directly onto the invitation. Or you can achieve a much nicer effect by using the artwork as a template for your own versions of the picnic foods and label made with assorted colored papers.

8. Apply glue to the back of each cut-out food item and carefully insert into the zigzag incision on the brown craft paper invitation. Arrange the food items as shown in the finished invitation.

9. Cut out the grass out of Template B. Apply glue to the back of the grass cutout and paste it along the top of the checkered picnic blanket and on either side of the brown paper bag as shown in the finished invitation.

10. Cut a 6¼" (15.5 cm) square piece of green paper (or in any other color you prefer).

11. Apply glue to the back of the invitation and paste it in the center of the square green paper. Tip: You can use the back of the invitation to write an additional message.

12. Take the cut-out label from Template B (or one that you've made) and paste it in the center of the front of the 6½" (17 cm) square brown craft paper envelope. Write the name of the recipient on the label if it's not already printed.

Pack a picnic lunch & meet us by the bay!

Golden Gate Park at noon on June 20

RSVP (415) 831-5500

BRING A BAG LUNCH

To Caroline

ARTIST: ANNA HERRICK

materials

- downloadable templates: Brown Bag Lunch, Picnic Materials (See page 18 for instructions.)
- brown craft paper
- white paper
- assorted colored paper
- 6½" (17 cm) square brown craft paper envelope
- metal ruler
- craft knife
- personal computer
- scanner
- graphic design software (Adobe Photoshop, Illustrator, or other)
- inkjet or laser printer
- glue stick
- scissors

Fits in a 6½" (17 cm) square envelope

Dial-a-Greeting

This card keeps on giving for an entire year. Set the arrow to the appropriate holiday and you're off the hook for the next 365 days.

materials

- ~ downloadable template: Dial-a-Greeting *(See page 18 for instructions.)*
- ~ 8 ½" × 11" (22 × 28 cm) chartreuse green card stock
- ~ ¾" (2 cm) paper fasteners
- ~ computer
- ~ page layout program *(Quark XPress)*
- ~ scanner
- ~ inkjet or laser printer
- ~ craft knife
- ~ cutting mat
- ~ screw punch

Fits in a 6" (15 cm) square envelope

Dial-a-Greeting Directions:
Keep this card for the next 365 days.
Turn the arrow to the appropriate holiday and know
we'll be thinking of you on your special day.

(and I guess we're off the hook until next year).

happy birthday
happy hanukkah
happy valentine's
happy mother's
happy father's
happy whatever
happy anniversary
merry christmas
DIAL-A-GREETING

1. Download the Dial-a-Greeting image to your computer.

2. Create an 8½" × 11" (22 × 28 cm) page in your layout program.

3. Place the template image on your page.

4. Print the page on the green card stock.

5. Cut out the arrow and circle with the craft knife and punch a hole with the screw punch in the center of each.

6. Place the arrow over the circle and place a paper fastener through the holes. Splay and flatten points on the back of the card.

VARIATION » *Design a circular theme card of your own for one particular topic such as Dial-a-Mood with words such as "happy," "sad," or "tired" on it.*

A Show of Hands

Inexpensive stock photography and a little computer wizardry make this a stunning and educational birthday card.

1. Purchase a high-resolution sign language image from a stock agency. The images generally run between $1.00-$3.00 (about £1.5) per image.

2. Create a new 8 ½" × 7" (22 × 18 cm) page layout document.

3. Divide page in half vertically and create a full bleed black box on the lower half of the page measuring 8 ½" × 3 ½" (22 × 9 cm).

4. Make a picture box for each of the images that spell out happy birthday and place in two rows as shown in the photo, leaving a blank space between the letter "b" and the word "day."

5. Typeset the word "enjoy" in the blank space.

6. Print, then trim the card out.

7. Score and fold in half vertically.

materials

~ 8 ½" × 11" (22 × 28 cm) uncoated photo paper for inkjet or laser printer

~ page layout program (Quark XPress)

~ computer

~ craft knife

~ metal ruler

~ color inkjet or laser printer

Fits in a # 10 envelope

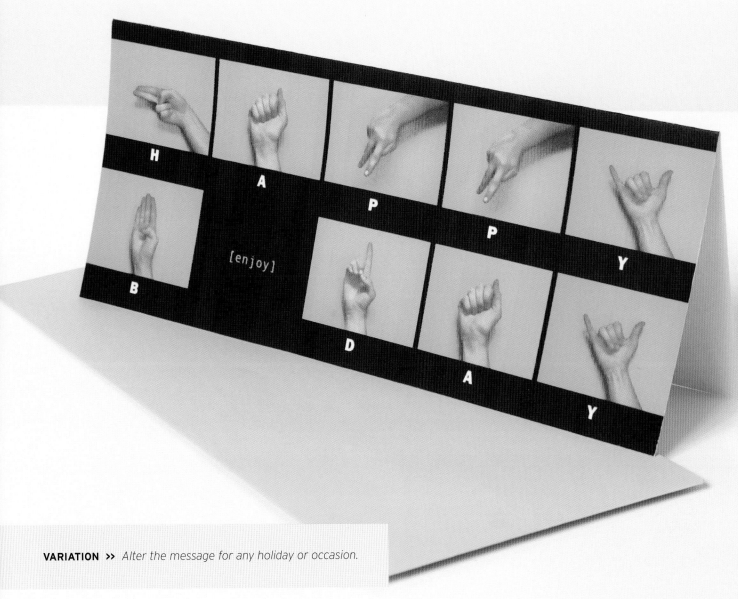

VARIATION >> *Alter the message for any holiday or occasion.*

materials

~ downloadable templates:
  Movin' and Groovin'
  *(See page 18 for
  instructions.)*

~ color paper
  CD envelopes

~ photo-quality
  inkjet paper

~ laser or inkjet
  compatible paper
  in assorted
  bright colors

~ computer

~ layout software
  (Photoshop)

~ Zapf Dingbats
  or Wood
  Ornaments
  postscript fonts

~ glue stick

~ craft knife

ARTIST: ANNA HERRICK

Movin' 'n' a Groovin' CD Cards

A circular window on a CD envelope makes a perfect frame for a bold graphic design.

1. Download and open the Movin' and Groovin' templates.

2. To make the interior of the card, create a new layout document and save as Interior. Set the page dimensions at 4 ¾" × 9 ½" (12 × 24 cm). Set a horizontal guideline at 4 ¾" (12 cm) from the top of the page, so the page is evenly divided into two square halves stacked on top of each other.

3. Draw a circle 4" (10 cm) in diameter and place in the center of the bottom half of the page. This is where you'll write a note once the card is finished.

4. Fill circle with the color of your choice. Tip: Be mindful of the color you choose because it will be printed on colored paper. For example, a blue circle printed on yellow paper will result in a green circle. Bright and light colors work best for this step. For an alternate design, color the area around the circle, and leave the circle blank.

5. Place colored paper of choice in your laser or inkjet printer.

6. Set up the document to print with crop marks. Print the document and set aside.

7. To make the design for the front exterior of the card, set up another document and save as "Exterior" with the same dimensions and guideline.

8. Choose Zaph Dingbats or Wood Ornaments fonts.

9. Type a 350-point asterisk-shaped symbol.

10. Rasterize the type, which means to convert it from a type element into a graphic element that can be altered in different ways. Tip: If you are not experience using Photoshop software, it may be much easier to skip the last three steps and use the downloadable templates.

11. Place a symbol of your choice in the center of the top half of the page.

12. Using the paint bucket tool, color sections of the symbol as you wish.

13. If desired, pick a color to surround the symbol.

14. Place a sheet of bright white paper into your laser or inkjet printer.

15. Set up the document to print with crop marks. Print the document.

16. Align the crop marks on the two printed pages back to back by holding them against a window or light table. The circle should be on the bottom half and the symbol should be on the top half. Glue the backs of the pages together. Using the crop marks as a guide, trim the glued pages.

17. Fold in half, so that the symbol is on the front of the folded card.

18. Place in the CD envelope with the color of your choice.

TIP ›› *You can make your own designs using symbols found in Zapf Dingbats, Wood Ornaments, and other symbol font packages. Or you can simply scan and use the templates provided online.*

OPTIONAL STEP FOR THE MATCHBOOKS >> *Create a separate document 3¾" × 11" (10 × 28 cm). Draw eight vertical lines ¼" (6 mm) apart from one another and center them on the page. These lines should be 10" (25 cm) long and start ½" (1 cm) from the top of the page. Write the word Dear in 9-point American Typewriter font on the first line. Print this on the back side of matchbook graphic sheet.*

The Perfect Match

These retro matchbook cover cards offer a variety of vintage graphics that are reminders of yesteryear's food and travel.

For the matchbooks:

1. Download and open one of the Perfect Match Images 1-5 into your scanning program. It should measure 3 ¾" × 11" (10 × 28 cm).

2. Print the template onto the sheet of watercolor paper, using the centered option in your printer setup dialog box.

3. Trim the card out and fold it like a real matchbook cover, making sure to staple the bottom flap of the card.

For the matchbox lid:

1. Follow steps 1-2 for the top of the box.

2. Glue the orange Indian Text Orange Cubes paper to the box lid and trim to fit.

3. Cut the pattern out and glue the tabs for the box lid.

4. Open the Perfect Match Top template in your scanning program and print it onto the sticker paper.

5. Trim out the sticker with the rotary trimmer, center it, and adhere it to the box lid.

For the matchbox bottom:

1. Open the Perfect Match Bottom template in your scanning program and print it onto a sheet of white paper.

2. Trim the white paper to the size of the template and trace the template onto the bristol board.

3. Cut the pattern out and glue the tabs for the bottom of the box.

materials

for the matchbooks

~ downloadable template: Perfect Match Top *(See page 18 for instructions.)*

~ watercolor paper trimmed to 8 ½" × 14" (22 × 36 cm)

~ computer

~ scanner

~ scanning program *(Photoshop)*

~ color printer

~ metal ruler

~ craft knife

~ cutting mat

~ stapler and staples

for the matchbox

~ downloadable template: Perfect Match Bottom *(See page 18 for instructions.)*

~ downloadable templates: Perfect Match Images 1-5 *(See page 18 for instructions.)*

~ 8 ½" × 11" (22 × 28 cm) bristol board

~ Indian Text Orange Cubes decorative paper

~ white adhesive-backed printer paper

~ craft or PVA glue

~ paintbrush

~ rotary trimmer with deckled edge

Fits in 4 ½" × 5 ½" (11 × 14 cm) envelope

materials

~ downloadable template: Lollipop Stationery *(See page 18 for instructions.)*

~ 8 ½" × 11" (22 × 28 cm) superfine white text paper *(green shown here)*

~ 8 ½" × 11" (22 × 28 cm) inkjet compatible vellum

~ #8660 clear mailing labels *(Avery)*

~ computer

~ word processing program *(MS Word)*

~ color printer

Fits in a #10 envelope

Lollipop Stationery and Mailing Labels

Use this simple stationery for business or personal correspondence.
Change the paper in your printer to make it either formal or funky.

For the stationery:

1. Create an 8 ½" × 11" (22 × 28 cm) document in your word processing program. Place the Lollipop Stationery template in your page about 1" (3 cm) from the top and ½" (1 cm) from the left-hand side of the page.

2. Set the type for the letterhead. For the names, we used 10.5-point Square Slab 711 Medium BT spaced out with a tracking of 35, all lowercase letters. For the address line, we used 8-point Verdana, all lower-case. Add some space and draw a line to separate the address line from the email address.

3. Print the letterhead onto the white text and green vellum sheets.

For the stickers:

1. In your MS Word document, you will find the preset label layouts under the Tools ➡ Letters and Mailings ➡ Envelopes and Labels ➡ Labels tab ➡ Options menu. Use the Avery label making template number 8660. Place the graphic on the page (about ⅛" [3 mm] from the bottom of the label) and set the names over the address line (don't put the email address on the labels). Print the labels onto the label paper.

TIP » *The vellum has a tendency to stick together, so you may want to feed the sheets individually through the printer or place plain white sheets of paper in between each of the sheets of vellum.*

ETC »

Resources, Contributors, About the Author, Acknowledgments

Resources ⌄⌄

A. C. Moore
www.acmoore.com

The Art Store
A Blick Company
www.artstore.com

CardBlanks *(Canada and US)*
www.cardblanks.com

Captured Elements
www.capturedelements.com

Charmed Cards & Crafts *(UK)*
www.charmedcardsand-
crafts.co.uk

Cheddar Stamper *(UK)*
www.cheddarstamper.co.uk

Crafts, Etc.
www.craftsetc.com

Create for Less
www.createforless.com

Creative Crafts *(UK)*
www.creativecrafts.co.uk

Curry's Art Store *(Canada)*
www.currys.com

Eckersley's Arts, Crafts, and
Imagination *(New South
Wales, Queensland, South
Australia, and Victoria)*
www.eckersleys.com.au

Fabric Place
www.fabricplace.com

Graphigro *(France)*
www.graphigro.com

HobbyCraft Group
Limited *(UK)*
www.hobbycraft.co.uk

Jo-Ann Fabrics
www.joann.com

John Lewis *(UK)*
www.johnlewis.co.uk

Kate's Paperie
www.katespaperie.com

Lazar StudioWerx Inc
(Canada)
www.lazarstudiowerx.com

Making Memories
www.makingmemories.com

Memory Creators
www.memorycreators.com

Memory Villa
www.memoryvilla.com

Michaels, The Arts
& Craft Store
www.michaels.com

OfficeMax
www.officemax.com

Paper Source
www.paper-source.com

Pearl Art and Craft Supply
www.pearlpaint.com

Staples
www.staples.com

Target
www.target.com

T. N. Lawrence & Son Ltd *(UK)*
www.lawrence.co.uk

Deborah Baskin
Blue Sky Development
deborahbaskin@comcast.net
Deborah is an architect living
in Somerville, MA.

Carolynn DeCillo
Carolynnd@comcast.net
Carolynn is a graphic designer living
in Somerville, MA.

Jeanmarie Fiocchi-Marden
Jeanmarie is an art educator and graphic
designer living in Spring Lake, NJ.

Anna Herrick
Anna Herrick is an illustrator, graphic
designer, and craft fanatic living in
Somerville, MA.

Katie Lipsitt
Katie Lipsitt is an artist and art
teacher living in Los Angeles, CA.

Mary Lawler
Lawler Design
mary.lawler@verizon.net
Mary Lawler is a graphic designer
and mixed-media collage artist in
South Hadley, MA.

Stephanie McAtee
Captured Elements,LLC.
steph.mcatee@capturedelements.com
Stephanie is a product designer and
instructor living in Kansas City, MO.

Andy McFadden
Andreamcf@aol.com
Andy is an artist and project coordinator
living in Havertown, PA.

Kevin Miller
kevinm@pohlypartners.com
Kevin is a creative director at a gigantic
communications company and lives in
Boston. He does not have any cats and most
days is generally on the fence about design.

Mary Kreindel
mkreindel@quinnprinting.com
Mary is a print representative and fine
artist living in Newton, MA.

Allyson Ross
NickowitzRoss Design
nickowitzross@comcast.net
Allyson is a graphic designer and mother
of Luka living in Cambridge, MA.

Sandra Salamony
ssalamony@SkyandTelescope.com
Artist and designer Sandra Salamony is the
author (with Maryellen Driscoll) of *The
Gardener's Craft Companion* (Rockport
Publishers, 2002) as well as other books on
fine crafting. Her art-and-craft projects have
been featured in many books, magazines,
newspapers, and online publications.

Jeanine Stein
jsteinelson@yahoo.com
Jeannine teaches bookbinding and paper
crafts in Los Angeles, CA.

⌃Contributors

About the Author

Laura McFadden is a freelance art director living in Somerville, Massachusetts. She is a former design director for *Inc.* magazine. She currently runs her own graphic design studio, Laura McFadden Design, Inc. She has contributed to various craft books and magazines for publishers such as Rockport Publishers, Martingale & Company, and *Handcraft Illustrated*. She is coauthor with April Paffrath of *The Artful Bride: Simple, Handmade Wedding Projects* and *The Artful Bride: Wedding Invitations: A Stylish Bride's Guide to Simple, Handmade Wedding Correspondence*.

Acknowledgments

Many, many thanks to all the great folks at Rockport who have supported me on this book. In particular, I'd like to thank Mary Ann Hall, who has continued to give me one lucky break after another and is always open to new ideas. I'd also like to thank Regina Grenier, with her keen sense of style and sage design advice. Thank you to publisher, Winnie Prentiss; project manager, Betsy Gammons; copy editor, Kristy Mulkern; and photographer, Allan Penn.

Much love and gratitude to Anna Herrick, who contributed volumes of stunning work to this book and is always a great source of inspiration and wit. Also, tons of thanks to my extremely tolerant friends Deborah Baskin, Carolynn DeCillo, and Jeanmarie Fiocchi-Marden, who have had to listen to me blather on about ideas and contributed some of their own fabulous ones. And, on top of all of that, thank you to contributors Mary Lawler, Stephanie McAtee, Sandra Salamony, Jeanine Stein; my sister-in-law, Andrea McFadden, and my friends Kevin Miller, Mary Kreindel, and Allyson Nickowitz Ross.